Core Computer Science from Scratch Without Traditional Academic Pathways

Self-Guided Foundations for Programmers, Analysts, Builders, and Beginners

AF872641

Renee Montoya

Table of Contents

INTRODUCTION 5

CHAPTER I: Understanding Computer Science Fundamentals.....6

Understanding What Computer Science Really Is 6

Developing Computational Thinking and Problem-Solving Skills 12

Exploring How Computers Process Information 18

Building a Self-Directed Learning Mindset 25

CHAPTER II: Learning Programming from the Ground Up 33

Understanding Programming Logic and Core Concepts 33

Working with Variables, Data Types, and Control Structures 40

Mastering Functions, Modular Design, and Code Organization 48

Developing Effective Debugging and Testing Habits 55

CHAPTER III: Exploring Essential Computer Science Disciplines 64

Understanding Data Structures and Algorithms 64

Learning Computer Architecture and Operating Systems 71

Exploring Databases, Networking, and Internet Technologies 79

Understanding Software Engineering Principles and Development Practices 87

CHAPTER IV: Applying Computer Science Through Practical Projects 96

Designing Real-World Software Applications 96

Working with APIs, Libraries, and Development Tools 102

Building Web, Desktop, and Automation Projects 110

Managing Projects with Version Control and Collaboration Practices 116

CHAPTER V: Advancing Toward Professional Computer Science Skills 123

Learning Artificial Intelligence and Emerging Technologies 123

Strengthening Cybersecurity Awareness and Secure Development 130

Creating a Professional Portfolio and Continuous Learning Strategy 137

Preparing for Careers, Freelancing, and Lifelong Growth in Computer Science 146

CONCLUSION 156

INTRODUCTION

It is no longer necessary to follow the conventional academic path to learn computer science. Motivated learners can now develop strong technical knowledge through self-directed study and regular practice thanks to an abundance of materials, useful tools, and online communities. Success comes from a person's ability to think logically, solve issues, and apply new ideas to actual circumstances rather than from where they start. A methodical approach helps break down difficult topics into digestible courses that progressively increase competence and confidence.

This book emphasizes practical understanding over rote memorization while guiding students through the fundamental ideas underpinning computer science. Instead of assuming prior knowledge, it presents key concepts gradually, enabling novices to gain a firm understanding of programming, computational thinking, algorithms, software development, and the technologies that underpin contemporary computing. Every subject is covered in a logical order so that each new idea builds organically upon what has already been learned.

Beyond technical proficiency, the trip fosters curiosity, perseverance, and self-directed learning. Through practical projects and experiments, readers will learn methods for mastering difficult subjects, overcoming challenges, and continually improving. The objective is to acquire practical skills and theoretical knowledge that apply to many programming languages and technologies. Anyone can gain the confidence to develop useful software, solve practical problems, and advance in the rapidly changing field of computing by adhering to this learning path with commitment and consistency.

CHAPTER I
Understanding Computer Science Fundamentals

Understanding What Computer Science Really Is

The methodical study of computing, information, and the techniques machines use to analyze, store, communicate, and alter data is known as computer science. Computer science is far more than just writing code, even though many people equate it with programming. It includes the theories, concepts, and useful methods that describe how computers handle information, solve issues, and facilitate a wide range of contemporary activities. Computer science lays the groundwork for a variety of technologies, including cloud computing, artificial intelligence, cellphones, and websites. Realizing that computer science is both an engineering practice and a scientific discipline is the first step towards comprehending what it really is. To construct systems that increase productivity, automate tasks, and open up completely new possibilities for communication, commerce, healthcare, education, entertainment, and scientific research, it integrates logical reasoning, mathematical thinking, creativity, and practical problem-solving.

The idea of computation is central to computer science. The process of following a set of instructions to solve a problem or achieve a desired outcome is called computation. Before the invention of electronic computers, people carried out calculations by hand using predetermined methods. Machines capable of performing these tasks far more quickly and precisely than humans were developed as technology improved. Even while modern computers can do billions of calculations per second, they still need human-written, meticulously crafted instructions. These instructions, sometimes referred to as programs, direct computers in all of their operations, from analyzing vast amounts of scientific data to displaying letters on a screen.

The emphasis on problem-solving in computer science is one of its distinguishing features. Instead of focusing solely on machines, computer scientists seek methods to break down complex problems into smaller components and develop logical solutions that computers can effectively implement. Careful preparation, critical thought, and methodical analysis are necessary for this process. The first step of any software program, operating system, website, mobile application, or intelligent system is to identify a problem and choose the most effective computational solution. The fundamental method entails converting a real-world problem into a series of exact computational procedures, regardless of the objective—organizing financial records, forecasting weather patterns, recommending movies, or operating autonomous vehicles.

Although programming is a significant component of computer science, it accounts for only a small percentage of the discipline. Writing instructions in programming languages that computers can understand or convert into machine processes is the practical act of programming. On the other hand, computer science studies the more general ideas that underlie programming, such as algorithms, data structures, software architecture, computational theory, and system design. Someone can learn to develop programs without fully understanding the scientific concepts that underpin their scalability, efficiency, and reliability. The deeper understanding required to assess various strategies, maximize performance, and create software that keeps working well even as complexity rises is provided by computer science.

Because they specify the exact procedures for completing a given task, algorithms are essential to computer science. Whether sorting names alphabetically, searching the internet for information, compressing images, encrypting messages, or identifying faces in photos, every computer function depends on one or more algorithms. A well-designed algorithm uses the least amount of time and computer power while producing accurate results. Because even minor enhancements can significantly boost the efficiency of large systems, computer scientists devote considerable effort to understanding algorithms. Whether an application responds quickly or takes too long to process data is frequently determined by selecting the right algorithm.

Data is another fundamental idea in computer science. The main purposes of computers are information processing, storage, retrieval, and communication. Numbers, text, photos, audio, video, and sensor readings are just a few of the various formats that data can take. Computer science investigates the representation of data within computers, its efficient organization, and its rapid access when required. Different processing and storing strategies are needed for different kinds of data. Businesses can evaluate consumer behavior, hospitals can keep track of medical records, researchers can investigate patterns in the climate, and governments can provide public services more effectively when information is managed effectively.

In every computing system, computer hardware and software function as complementary parts. Physical devices like CPUs, memory, storage drives, keyboards, displays, and networking equipment are referred to as hardware. The instructions that tell the hardware what to do are called software. Because successful computing depends on their relationship, computer science studies both elements. Without well-designed software, a powerful processor cannot accomplish significant tasks, and sophisticated software cannot function well without dependable hardware. Knowing how these components work together provides important insights into resource management, system performance, and technological constraints.

Network communication between computers is another area of study in computer science. Interconnected systems that share data via local and international networks are essential to modern life. One of computer science's greatest accomplishments is the internet itself, which connects billions of devices and enables nearly instantaneous data sharing. Communication protocols, routing strategies, security precautions, and distributed computing approaches that provide dependable information transmission are examples of networking principles. Email, online banking, video conferencing, cloud computing, social media platforms, and a host of other everyday digital services are all supported by these ideas.

Because digital information is so crucial to governmental, business, and personal activity, security has grown in importance within computer science. Computer scientists provide methods to defend systems from fraud, malware, illegal access, and cyberattacks. Risk management, secure programming techniques, encryption, and authentication all help to protect sensitive data. As technology continues to permeate every part of life, safeguarding digital systems is crucial for preserving financial stability, privacy, and public confidence. For computer professionals, security is therefore both a technological difficulty and an ethical obligation.

The focus on abstraction is another characteristic that sets computer science apart. By focusing on key aspects and temporarily ignoring superfluous complexity, abstraction simplifies complex systems. This idea enables engineers and programmers to create complex programs without having to comprehend every internal component at once. Programming languages translate machine instructions into intelligible code, operating systems conceal hardware complexity from application developers, and software libraries offer reusable solutions for routine tasks. Despite growing technological complexity, abstraction makes modern software development comprehensible and facilitates productive collaboration among huge teams.

Despite their close relationship, computer science and information technology are not the same. The deployment, upkeep, and maintenance of computer systems inside businesses is the core focus of information technology. Information technology specialists build systems, set up networks, manage servers, and assist users with technical issues. In contrast, computer science places a strong emphasis on creating new technologies, creating software, researching algorithms, and expanding computational understanding. Although many professions use aspects of both fields, knowing the difference enables students to recognize the more comprehensive scientific basis that computer science offers.

Computer science has an impact on almost every industry. Healthcare companies use advanced software to support medical research, manage patient information, and diagnose illnesses. For safe electronic transactions, investment analysis, and fraud detection, financial institutions rely on complex algorithms. Manufacturers use automation systems to improve product quality and production efficiency. Educational institutions use digital learning platforms to increase global access to knowledge. Scientists use high-performance computing to simulate complex physical phenomena, analyze genetic data, and model climate change. Specialized software that boosts creativity and productivity also helps artists, musicians, architects, and filmmakers.

One of the areas of computer science that is expanding the fastest is artificial intelligence. Intelligent systems learn from data, identify patterns, and make predictions or draw conclusions based on experience rather than merely executing predefined instructions. Machine learning algorithms analyze large volumes of data to improve performance gradually. Applications include robotics, autonomous cars, medical diagnostics, recommendation systems, speech recognition, and language translation. Even though artificial intelligence frequently garners significant public attention, it remains firmly anchored in fundamental computer science concepts such as algorithms, probability, optimization, and data representation.

Learning computer science involves more than just learning software commands and programming syntax by heart. Developing logical thinking, perseverance, curiosity, and a desire to use methodical experimentation to solve difficult problems are all necessary for success. Because troubleshooting and improving solutions enhance analytical abilities, mistakes are an integral element of the learning process. Along the road, every successful programmer and computer scientist runs into mistakes, strange behaviors, and challenging ideas. Understanding the causes of issues, testing potential fixes, and consistently enhancing technical expertise and problem-solving skills are all necessary for progress.

In the end, computer science is the study of how to solve significant problems by representing, processing, communicating, and transforming information. It enables people to create technologies that enhance lives and expand human capabilities by fusing scientific research with practical innovation. Every digital system, from the biggest global computing infrastructure to the tiniest mobile application, embodies the fundamentals of computer science. By grasping these concepts, students can develop, enhance, and modify technology to address new difficulties in addition to using it efficiently. A strong grasp of computer science provides a durable foundation for lifelong learning, career development, and significant contributions to an increasingly digital world as technology continues to advance at an astounding rate.

Developing Computational Thinking and Problem-Solving Skills

One of the most crucial parts of studying computer science is developing computational thinking and problem-solving abilities. The capacity to reason and approach issues methodically is a timeless skill, even as programming languages, software tools, and technology continue to advance. Writing computer programs and utilizing cutting-edge technologies are not the only applications of computational thinking. Rather, it is a methodical approach to scenario analysis, pattern recognition, information organization, and the creation of workable solutions that both computers and people can execute. It is useful not only in computing but also in science, engineering, business, education, healthcare, and daily decision-making because it instills in students a disciplined approach that enables them to solve complex problems effectively.

The first step in computational thinking is recognizing that many large, complex situations can be better understood by decomposing them into smaller, more manageable components. Decomposition is the term for this process, which enables people to concentrate on one aspect of a problem at a time rather than being overtaken by its entire complexity. For instance, developing an online shopping application entails numerous distinct activities, such as coordinating deliveries, maintaining inventory, processing payments, managing customer accounts, and designing the user interface. Developers split the project into smaller modules that may be separately planned, tested, and improved rather than trying to build the full system at once. This methodical approach reduces uncertainty, streamlines development, and improves collaboration among team members.

Pattern recognition is another crucial component of computational thinking. Finding similarities between problems and circumstances that have already been resolved enables the reuse of existing knowledge and methods. To adapt tried-and-true solutions rather than starting from scratch, seasoned programmers frequently identify familiar structures in novel situations. For example, a lot of applications need to sort data, manage collections of records, validate user input, or search for information. Because they can use well-established algorithms and programming techniques in a wide range of circumstances, learners become more efficient once they identify these recurrent patterns. By pushing students to spot connections, patterns, and recurrent behaviors in data and systems, pattern recognition also enhances analytical thinking.

Another essential idea that facilitates efficient computational thinking is abstraction. Focusing on the most crucial aspects of a subject while temporarily disregarding less important parts is known as abstraction. Large volumes of information are present in every real-world problem, yet not all of the details are pertinent to the solution. People can make simplified models that are simpler to comprehend and solve by determining the key features. When creating software for a banking system, for instance, developers prioritize client accounts, transactions, balances, and security over irrelevant personal data. By eliminating needless complexity, this selective emphasis keeps systems efficient, manageable, and structured. Because each component has a distinct function, abstraction also makes software easier to maintain.

One of the key elements of computational thinking is algorithm design. An algorithm is a logical set of instructions designed to carry out a certain activity or solve a particular problem. Each computer program is made up of one or more algorithms that specify how data will be handled. Effective algorithm design necessitates meticulous preparation, logical thinking, and an awareness of efficiency. A well-designed algorithm should minimize needless steps, memory utilization, and processing time while yielding accurate results. Students are encouraged to think carefully before creating code as they learn to construct algorithms, which lowers errors and improves the quality of their answers. Additionally, this practice emphasizes the value of preparation as opposed to depending only on trial and error.

Because computers carry out instructions exactly as they are stated, logical reasoning is essential to computational thinking. Computers are unable to deduce missing information or decipher ambiguous instructions, in contrast to humans. Each instruction needs to be clear, comprehensive, and coherent. This requirement teaches students to properly organize their ideas and prepare for the many scenarios that can arise during execution. For instance, developers must take into account valid scores, missing data, inaccurate input, and exceptional cases when creating a system for computing student grades.

They develop more dependable software that functions properly under a variety of circumstances by considering every eventuality. This methodical approach strengthens analytical abilities that are useful far beyond programming.

Instead of depending solely on intuition, computer scientists use a methodical approach to solve problems. Clearly describing the issue and comprehending its requirements constitute the first stage. Many failed projects are not caused by poor programming, but rather by a misinterpretation of the real issue to be resolved. Following the identification of the issue, pertinent data are collected, goals are set, and potential limitations are considered. The following step is creating one or more prospective solutions, assessing their advantages and disadvantages, choosing the best strategy, and carefully putting it into practice. Ultimately, the solution is tested, modified, and tweaked until it achieves the intended goals. This methodical approach promotes critical thinking and minimizes expensive development errors.

By pushing people to challenge assumptions, assess evidence, and consider different options, critical thinking enhances computational thinking. Effective problem solvers consider several options before making a choice, rather than settling on the first one that comes to mind. They assess performance trade-offs, analyze several algorithms, and decide which strategy best meets the project's objectives. For instance, one algorithm might run faster but use more memory, while another might save memory but take longer to process. Developers can select solutions that best fit the unique needs of each application by being aware of these trade-offs. Thus, critical thinking facilitates improved decision-making at every stage of the software development process.

Despite being a crucial part of computational thinking, creativity is frequently overlooked in discussions of computer science. Innovative concepts and creative methods are often needed to solve complicated challenges. While logical reasoning and algorithms provide structure, creativity enables people to develop original applications, enhance existing systems, and find more effective ways to perform tasks. Combining well-known ideas in novel and creative ways leads to many technical innovations. Additionally, creative thinking promotes experimentation and ongoing development by assisting developers in adapting when conventional solutions prove inadequate. Instead of seeing computer science as a strict technical discipline, students should see it as a field that values both creativity and accuracy.

Another important trait that computational thinking fosters is persistence. Seldom are complex problems solved perfectly or right away. Unexpected mistakes, competing constraints, inadequate requirements, and technological difficulties that necessitate frequent testing and rewriting are common in programming projects. Successful students recognize that failure is not a sign of weakness but rather a normal element of the problem-solving process. Every error yield valuable information that directs future development. It takes perseverance and resolves to debug, improve algorithms, and maximize performance. These encounters gradually build resilience and self-assurance, allowing people to tackle increasingly challenging tasks with greater poise and expertise.

Additionally, computational thinking underscores the importance of evaluating solutions after they are implemented. Even if a program yields accurate results, it may still need improvement if it runs too slowly, uses too many resources, or is hard to maintain. Thus, in addition to accuracy, developers assess efficiency, readability, scalability, and dependability. They take into account the solution's capacity to handle more data, adapt to evolving needs, and eventually integrate with other systems. Instead of settling for merely functional results, this emphasis on ongoing review promotes lifelong improvement. Additionally, it teaches students that intelligent design and continuous improvement drive the evolution of high-quality software.

Computational thinking has many real-world uses outside of software development. To increase operational effectiveness, examine consumer behavior, and streamline decision-making procedures, business experts employ organized problem-solving techniques. Scientists use computational thinking to simulate complicated systems, interpret experimental data, and model natural occurrences. To manage patient records, interpret medical data, and support clinical decisions, healthcare professionals employ systematic thinking. While educators use computational thinking to plan lessons and assess students' development, engineers create dependable systems by breaking down big tasks into smaller, more manageable parts. Even routine tasks like making trip plans, handling money, setting up calendars, or cooking require dissecting issues into manageable chunks, identifying trends, and coming to rational conclusions.

By exposing people to a variety of viewpoints and different strategies, collaborative problem-solving further improves computational thinking. Seldom can a single developer finish a large software project. Rather, groups collaborate on requirements analysis, architectural design, feature implementation, code review, and system testing. Clear communication, rational explanations of ideas, and the ability to assess constructive criticism are all necessary for productive teamwork. When team members combine their unique experiences and knowledge, they frequently find superior solutions. Thus, mastering the art of communicating technical concepts accurately is crucial to developing strong computational thinking abilities.

Computational thinking is becoming more and more important in almost every job due to modern technologies. Robotics, data science, cloud computing, cybersecurity, and artificial intelligence all rely on methodical approaches to problem-solving. Employers are increasingly looking for people who can assess complex problems, develop logical solutions, and adapt to rapidly evolving technologies as industries undergo digital transformation. Regardless of which programming languages, software platforms, or technological tools gain popularity in the future, computational thinking offers a flexible, enduring basis. It gives students long-lasting abilities that facilitate lifelong learning throughout their careers.

In the end, mastering computational thinking and problem-solving techniques entails adopting a methodical yet imaginative approach to understanding problems and developing practical solutions. These skills go beyond creating computer programs and become useful tools for solving issues in almost every facet of contemporary life. Through decomposition, pattern identification, abstraction, algorithm creation, logical reasoning, critical thinking, creativity, perseverance, and ongoing assessment, students gain the self-assurance to approach progressively challenging assignments with clarity and accuracy. These fundamental abilities will remain crucial for creativity, prudent decision-making, and long-term success in computer science and many other disciplines as technology advances, where critical thinking and real-world problem-solving are necessary.

Exploring How Computers Process Information

Due to their exceptional speed, accuracy, and consistency in processing information, computers have become essential instruments in modern life. Every digital job relies on the computer's capacity to accept, interpret, manipulate, store, and convey information, whether it is sending a message, streaming a video, analyzing scientific data, or executing intricate business applications. Because it illustrates the connection among hardware, software, and data, understanding how computers process information is a fundamental basis for learning computer science. Instead of seeing computers as enigmatic devices that merely generate output, students learn about the logical procedures that enable contemporary technology to perform millions or even billions of operations per second. This information enhances programming skills, strengthens problem-solving skills, and fosters a deeper understanding of the engineering concepts behind computing systems.

Data, or unprocessed facts that computers may receive and handle, is the first step in the information management process. Numbers, letters, symbols, pictures, sounds, movies, and signals gathered from sensors and other devices can all be considered forms of data. Any information must be represented in a way that computers can comprehend before they can operate with it. Computers use electrical impulses that represent only two possible states, whereas humans can naturally understand spoken words, written language, or visual imagery. Binary digits, or bits, which are represented by the integers zero and one, are frequently used to express these two states. In the end, all information processed by a computer is transformed into combinations of these binary values, regardless of its original form.

The basis of all digital computing is binary representation. Groups of bits can represent far more information than a single bit, which can only store one of two potential values. A byte, which is typically used to represent a single character like a letter, integer, or punctuation mark, consists of eight bits. Documents, photos, music, movies, and software programs are stored in larger collections of bytes. To process human-readable data, computers constantly convert it into binary form. The processed data is then converted back into human-readable formats. This conversion process occurs continuously during every interaction with digital devices, even though people seldom see it.

Information processing is mostly carried out by the central processing unit, also known as the CPU or processor. The processor, sometimes referred to as the computer's brain, performs calculations, executes commands, makes logical decisions, and facilitates communication among various hardware components. Every software program relies on the processor to execute its commands. Billions of tiny transistors that turn electrical impulses on and off at incredibly fast speeds are found in modern CPUs. Together, these transistors perform billions of operations per second, enabling computers to finish difficult jobs nearly instantly. The CPU is one of the most important parts of any computing device, as its efficiency and speed significantly impact the system's overall performance.

The instruction cycle is a continuous series used in information processing. This cycle entails retrieving an instruction from memory, decoding it to ascertain the appropriate operation, carrying out the instruction, and, if needed, storing the outcome. These actions frequently take place billions of times every second. The CPU obtains the next instruction from memory during the fetch stage. Specialized circuits decode the instruction and determine the necessary operation. Execution entails doing the desired computation, comparison, or data transfer. Any information that is produced is then either transferred to another hardware component or written back to memory. Software programs may perform increasingly complex operations without interruption thanks to this rapid repetition.

Because memory stores both data and instructions while the processor works, it plays an equally significant part in information processing. RAM, or random-access memory, is a type of temporary storage that enables the processor to access information quickly. When a program is started, its instructions and required data are loaded into RAM from permanent storage so that the CPU may access them quickly. RAM greatly enhances application performance since it offers far faster access than long-term storage systems. RAM is volatile memory, so when the computer loses power, its data is lost. RAM's transient nature sets it apart from permanent storage devices, which save data even after shutdown.

When a computer is turned off, the operating system, software programs, and user files are permanently stored on long-term storage devices. Solid-state drives rely on electronic memory chips with no moving elements, whereas traditional hard disk drives store data on rotating magnetic disks. Compared to conventional hard disks, solid-state drives often provide faster data access, reduced power consumption, and increased durability. All data is still encoded in binary form, regardless of the storage technique employed. Selected portions of stored data are moved into RAM as needed so the processor can access them quickly while the program is running.

The crucial software layer that controls the computer's information processing is the operating system. It serves as a bridge between users, software, and hardware. Software programs would have to interact directly with each hardware device in the absence of an operating system, significantly increasing complexity. Rather, the operating system coordinates CPU scheduling, memory allocation, file management, device communication, security enforcement, and user interaction. The operating system decides how best to distribute memory, CPU time, and other resources while several programs are running concurrently. Users can seamlessly transition between apps while preserving steady system performance thanks to this cooperation.

Information enters the computer system through input devices. Sources of input data include keyboards, mice, touchscreens, microphones, cameras, scanners, sensors, and network connections. Every input device transforms environmental signals or bodily activities into digital data that the computer can process. An electrical signal that corresponds to a particular binary code, for instance, is produced when a keyboard key is pressed. Similar to how microphones convert sound waves into digital audio samples, digital cameras convert light into numerical values that represent color and brightness. Computers may receive data from a variety of physical sources thanks to these conversion procedures.

Following information processing, output devices display the results in comprehensible formats. By transforming digital data into visual pictures, monitors display text, graphics, animations, and videos. While speakers translate electronic impulses into audible sound, printers convert binary data into tangible pages. How computers convey processed information is further expanded by contemporary virtual reality headsets, projectors, and specialized display technologies. These outcomes arise from intricate sequences of binary processes performed within the computer's core components, even though users experience them through familiar visual or audio representations.

The Arithmetic Logic Unit, or ALU, is a specialized part of the processor that performs arithmetic and logical operations commonly used in data processing. At the same time, logical operations compare values and establish connections such as equality, greater than, or less than; arithmetic operations include addition, subtraction, multiplication, and division. Because logical operations enable conditional instruction execution, they also aid decision-making in software programs. These basic mathematical and logical skills are necessary for every computation performed by financial software, every comparison made in a search engine, and every choice made by a game or an artificial intelligence application.

Effective communication between system components is just as important to information processing efficiency as processor performance. Data, addresses, and control signals are sent between the CPU, memory, storage devices, and peripheral hardware via buses. Rapid information flow throughout the system is made possible by high-speed buses, which minimize delays and enhance overall performance. Modern computers can process ever-larger amounts of data with shorter wait times because of ongoing improvements in hardware architecture.

Through the use of parallel processing techniques, modern CPUs significantly improve performance. Many processors include multiple cores that can execute separate tasks concurrently rather than just one instruction at a time. Applications may perform complicated computations more effectively thanks to multi-core processors, which divide tasks among multiple processing units. Large-scale data analysis, video editing, artificial intelligence, gaming, and scientific simulations all benefit greatly from parallel processing. To maximize the computational power available in contemporary systems, software developers are increasingly creating programs that use multiple processor cores.

By allowing computers to share data over local and international links, computer networks expand information processing beyond individual machines. Information may be shared almost immediately between computers situated anywhere in the globe thanks to networking technologies. This capacity is further increased by cloud computing, which enables distant servers to handle and store data on behalf of customers. Applications can distribute computational tasks across robust data centers with thousands of interconnected machines rather than relying solely on local hardware. In addition to supporting contemporary web services, collaborative applications, and large databases, this distributed method improves scalability, dependability, and accessibility.

Because digital information frequently contains important financial, organizational, and personal data, security is vital throughout the information processing cycle. Sensitive information can only be accessed by authorized users thanks to protective mechanisms including encryption, authentication, access control, and secure communication protocols. Computers constantly check permissions, monitor system activity, and identify potential threats during processing. The intricacy of contemporary computer systems is demonstrated by these security measures, which operate in tandem with routine processing activities without appreciably impairing the user experience.

Reliable information processing also benefits from error detection and correction. Data corruption may occasionally result from electrical interference, transmission mistakes, or storage problems in hardware components and communication systems. Computers use a variety of methods to identify discrepancies and automatically fix a wide range of problems before they have an impact on users. Reliability techniques that maintain data integrity during processing and communication are incorporated into memory systems, storage devices, and network protocols. These precautions are particularly crucial in vital sectors where precise information is crucial, such as banking, healthcare, aviation, and scientific research.

The amazing synergy of hardware, software, and data that underpins all digital technology is ultimately revealed when one investigates how computers interpret information. Every element plays a part in converting unprocessed data into useful outcomes, from binary representation and CPU execution to memory management, storage systems, input/output devices, networking, and security. By understanding these procedures, students can better understand how computers work, as well as the significance of effective programming, careful resource management, and system design in computer science. Programming, artificial intelligence, cybersecurity, data science, and many other fields that depend on the precise and effective manipulation of digital information can all be studied with a strong foundation, thanks to the fundamental principles of information processing, which hold even as computing technology advances.

Building a Self-Directed Learning Mindset

When pursuing computer science, developing a self-directed learning mentality is one of the most beneficial investments one can make. Every year, new programming languages, software frameworks, hardware advancements, and development techniques emerge due to the rapid evolution of technology. Therefore, it is rarely sufficient to stay informed and productive to rely only on formal schooling or infrequent training. People who learn to direct their own education are better able to adjust to change, pick up new skills on their own, and overcome obstacles in both their personal and professional lives. Self-directed learners are accountable for setting learning objectives, finding trustworthy sources, practicing regularly, assessing their progress, and making ongoing changes. With this kind of thinking, learning becomes a lifetime habit that fosters development in a constantly evolving technological environment.

Personal accountability is the first step towards self-directed learning. Independent learners understand that their growth depends mostly on their own activities rather than on waiting for someone else to assign lessons, explain every idea, or offer continuous inspiration. They are aware that learning necessitates perseverance, patience, and constant effort rather than outside pressure. This sense of ownership motivates students to seek solutions actively, pose insightful questions, and maintain their curiosity about new subjects. Personal accountability is particularly crucial in computer science, where discoveries are made regularly, and many useful skills are developed long before they are included in conventional educational programs or textbooks.

Self-directed learning is motivated by curiosity. Naturally, curious people research new technology, experiment with novel concepts, and learn how systems operate. They ask why something works the way it does and how it may be improved to gain a deeper understanding rather than taking information at face value. This practice is rewarded in computer science because almost all concepts relate to more general principles and real-world applications. The investigative attitude required for significant technical advancement is already being developed by a learner who is curious about how websites convey information, how search engines arrange billions of pages, or how artificial intelligence detects voice. Learning becomes an interesting process of exploration when one is curious.

Setting specific learning objectives gives the educational process focus and direction. Without clear goals, students frequently feel overwhelmed by the vast amount of available knowledge or sidetracked by rapidly evolving technologies. Good goals specify what has to be taught, why it's important, and how success will be assessed. For instance, a student may choose to grasp variables, loops, functions, and fundamental algorithms before moving on to more complex subjects rather than establishing a general goal like mastering programming. In addition to making difficult subjects easier to handle, breaking down more ambitious goals into smaller milestones fosters a sense of progress. Reaching each goal boosts self-esteem and promotes lifelong learning.

The development of an organized learning plan enhances self-directed learning even more. Successful learners benefit from structured schedules that set aside regular time for reading, practicing, reviewing, and reflecting, even though flexibility is still crucial. Because information develops gradually through repeated exposure and application, consistency is often more helpful than sporadic bursts of intense study. A reasonable daily or weekly schedule reduces the risk of burnout while helping topics become familiar over time. When maintained consistently over months or years, even a small amount of focused study time each day can lead to significant long-term progress.

Another crucial component of independent study is choosing trustworthy educational materials. A vast array of educational resources, such as books, online courses, manuals, research articles, tutorials, videos, and technical communities, is accessible online. Nevertheless, not all sources provide precise or coherent information. By taking into account the author's experience, publication quality, technical accuracy, and consistency with prior knowledge, self-directed learners acquire the capacity to assess trustworthiness. In general, official documents, respectable publications, reputable educational institutions, and seasoned professionals offer more reliable knowledge than unconfirmed opinions or inadequate courses. Acquiring the ability to distinguish between reliable and unreliable sources helps avoid confusion and provides a strong foundation for future development.

When opposed to passive observation, active learning greatly increases comprehension. Rarely does reading books or viewing educational videos result in long-lasting knowledge unless students put what they have learned into practice. Because programming, debugging, system design, and problem-solving all require practical experience, computer science places a special emphasis on them. Through hands-on experience, theoretical concepts are reinforced through writing code, experimenting with various solutions, updating pre-existing programs, and developing one's own projects. Each practical task highlights strengths and limitations and offers chances for more in-depth comprehension. Through active engagement, abstract knowledge is transformed into useful abilities that can be confidently utilized in real-world scenarios.

Because they offer insightful feedback rather than signaling failure, mistakes are essential to self-directed learning. Programming mistakes, false presumptions, and failed experiments frequently expose misunderstandings that could otherwise go unnoticed. Instead of seeing these losses as reasons to give up, independent learners see them as chances to improve their comprehension. Patience, analytical thinking, and resilience are developed through software debugging, understanding unexpected results, and rewriting failed solutions. Every adjustment leads to increased proficiency, proving that advancement frequently results from constant improvement rather than quick achievement. Long-term confidence and constant exploration are encouraged by this optimistic outlook on errors.

Independent learning is further improved by forming efficient problem-solving habits. Successful learners initially try to examine problems on their own, rather than looking for whole solutions right away. They identify the fundamental problem, consider potential causes, develop theories, test various strategies, and assess outcomes. This systematic approach lessens reliance on outside help while enhancing logical reasoning. Seeking advice is still beneficial when needed, but depending solely on pre-made solutions restricts true comprehension. Throughout a professional career, independent research fosters the self-assurance and ingenuity needed to tackle progressively challenging technological problems.

Effective self-directed learning also heavily depends on time management. Social media, entertainment platforms, incessant notifications, and conflicting obligations are just a few of the many distractions that modern learners must deal with. It takes deliberate preparation and strict study habits to stay focused. Concentration and productivity are increased by designating specific study times, reducing distractions, and giving important tasks top priority. Many students find that shorter, focused study sessions yield better results than longer, distracted sessions. Creating sustainable routines helps turn learning from an infrequent endeavor driven solely by deadlines or external expectations into a regular habit.

Another crucial activity that promotes ongoing development is reflection. Thoughtful students assess what they have learned, pinpoint unanswered issues, and think about how new information relates to earlier ideas after finishing a course, assignment, or study session. While highlighting areas that need more attention, reflective thinking strengthens comprehension. Students can track their development over time by taking notes, keeping learning journals, or analyzing finished work. Additionally, reflection fosters metacognition—the capacity to consider one's own learning process—which helps people improve their study techniques and become more capable, independent learners.

Long-term motivation is strengthened by gaining confidence through incremental success. Because of its sophisticated jargon, esoteric ideas, and quickly evolving technologies, computer science frequently seems overwhelming. However, as students complete increasingly difficult assignments, confidence grows organically. Measurable progress is demonstrated by finishing a personal software project, understanding a complex algorithm, developing a first program successfully, or addressing a challenging debugging challenge. These successes support the idea that sustained effort yields significant outcomes. Because it is based on proven skill, confidence derived from real success offers more incentive than fleeting encouragement.

One of the traits that still distinguishes self-directed learners is adaptability. Programming languages, development tools, hardware platforms, and software engineering techniques are all constantly changing due to technological breakthroughs. Adaptable learners embrace opportunities to broaden their knowledge and explore cutting-edge technologies rather than resisting change. They are aware that mastering a single software framework or programming language provides transferable skills that make learning new technologies easier in the future. Professionals can contribute successfully to cutting-edge initiatives and evolving industries while staying relevant over the course of extended careers thanks to flexibility.

Self-directed learning is further enhanced by involvement in learning groups. While independent learning places a strong emphasis on personal accountability, meaningful social connection speeds up development by offering a variety of viewpoints, helpful criticism, and shared experiences. Students can ask questions, share ideas, and work together on difficult problems through online discussion boards, open-source projects, technical conferences, study groups, and professional communities. While hearing other people's perspectives expands technical knowledge, explaining ideas to others strengthens one's own understanding. The advantages of group experience are combined with the strengths of individual study in a healthy collaboration.

Because learning computer science will always involve times of frustration and uncertainty, developing resilience is equally crucial. Challenging ideas, recurring programming mistakes, and unfamiliar technologies may momentarily slow progress. Self-directed learners understand that these difficulties are not permanent barriers but rather normal phases of development. They maintain patience, break down challenging issues into smaller, more manageable chunks, seek additional resources when needed, and keep practicing despite brief setbacks. This tenacity frequently sets effective learners apart from those who give up on their objectives too soon. Overcoming difficult situations develops both technical proficiency and emotional fortitude, which is advantageous in many facets of life.

Relying only on external rewards is considerably less efficient at sustaining long-term learning than maintaining internal motivation. Long-term academic accomplishment often stems from a genuine interest in understanding how technology works and developing meaningful solutions, even if grades, certifications, or professional opportunities may provide initial incentive. Solving challenges, creating practical applications, and expanding their knowledge are all sources of gratification for intrinsically motivated learners. Even when formal educational goals have been met, this internal feeling of purpose promotes ongoing inquiry. Lifelong curiosity becomes a dependable source of inspiration that fosters further growth at both the personal and professional levels.

In the end, developing a self-directed learning mindset enables people to take charge of their educational path and boldly adapt to a rapidly evolving technological environment. Learners acquire abilities that go well beyond computer science itself through self-responsibility, curiosity, organized preparation, active practice, introspective reflection, resilience, flexibility, and ongoing development. They develop the ability to learn new things on their own, approach new challenges methodically, and confidently embrace innovation. The capacity to learn efficiently becomes just as useful as knowledge itself as technology continues to advance at an unparalleled rate. A self-directed learning mentality ensures that development is a lifelong process, motivated by curiosity, self-control, perseverance, and the desire to turn knowledge into useful action, rather than being exclusively dependent on formal instruction.

CHAPTER II
Learning Programming from the Ground Up

Understanding Programming Logic and Core Concepts

The basis for being a successful programmer and computer scientist is an understanding of programming logic and fundamental ideas. It is crucial to comprehend the thinking process that enables software to solve issues before understanding the syntax of any programming language. Programming is the skill of creating logical instructions that allow a computer to carry out particular activities precisely and effectively. It is much more than just writing lines of code. Logical reasoning and basic programming concepts are the foundation of every successful application, from a basic calculator to an advanced artificial intelligence system. By grasping these ideas, students can produce reliable software, analyze complex problems, and confidently transition between programming languages.

The methodical process of analyzing a problem and determining the exact sequence of instructions needed to achieve a desired result is known as programming logic. Computers lack human intuition and the capacity to decipher ambiguous instructions. Each procedure needs to be fully, rationally, and clearly explained. Programmers are encouraged by this obligation to think methodically, foresee many scenarios, and arrange solutions so that computers can execute them without difficulty. Regardless of the programming language they choose, strong programming logic enables developers to create code that is easier to comprehend, maintain, and enhance over time.

The idea of problem solution is fundamental to programming. Finding a need or issue that technology can solve is the first step in any software project. Before writing any code, programmers examine the problem, whether the objective is to conduct financial transactions, automate tedious chores, organize information, or create interactive games. They identify the inputs, ascertain the anticipated consequences, identify any limitations, and create a logical procedure that converts the input into significant outcomes. Instead of just creating functional code, this analytical method ensures that programming remains focused on solving real-world problems.

The algorithm is one of the key ideas in programming. An algorithm is a meticulously crafted set of instructions that explains how to solve a specific problem. Because algorithms concentrate on logical processes rather than syntax, they exist irrespective of computer languages. For instance, regardless of whether it is implemented in Java, Python, C++, or another language, an algorithm for determining the greatest number in a list follows the same logical procedure. Before developing code, learning to design algorithms promotes meticulous planning and lowers the possibility of implementation errors. Prioritizing logical reasoning over memorization also improves problem-solving skills.

Programming languages facilitate human-computer communication. Programming languages give developers a more legible and structured way to communicate algorithms, even though computers can only comprehend machine language consisting of binary instructions. High-level programming languages make software development less error-prone and more efficient by using words, symbols, and structures that mimic human reasoning. All programming languages share basic ideas such as variables, expressions, conditions, loops, functions, and data structures, even though each has its own unique syntax and features. Understanding these fundamental ideas makes learning other programming languages much simpler because the underlying logic is always the same.

One of the most basic components of programming is a variable. A designated storage location used to store data that might change while a program is running is called a variable. Developers assign information to variables and change those values as needed, rather than entering particular values repeatedly throughout a program. Software can receive user input, perform computations, store temporary results, and manage application data effectively thanks to variables. Selecting relevant variable names also enhances code readability, making programs simpler to comprehend and update for both the original creator and any future collaborators.

By specifying the types of data that variables can hold, data types offer another crucial idea. Different processing and storing techniques are needed for different kinds of data. Integers for whole numbers, floating-point values for decimal figures, characters for individual symbols, strings for text, and Boolean values for true or false conditions are examples of common data types. Programmers can choose the best storage options, perform precise computations, and prevent errors caused by incompatible operations by having a solid understanding of data types. Additional specialized data types are frequently included in modern programming languages to facilitate complicated applications while preserving dependability and efficiency.

Programs may alter data and perform calculations using expressions and operators. While comparison operators assess relationships between values, arithmetic operators perform mathematical operations, including addition, subtraction, multiplication, and division. Several conditions are combined using logical operators to facilitate complex decision-making processes. When combined, these operators allow software to compute results, interpret data, and adapt to changing conditions. Because incorrect expressions can lead to unexpected outcomes, it is crucial to understand how operators interact and how expressions are evaluated.

Another fundamental idea that enables programs to react differently based on particular circumstances is decision-making. In the absence of decision-making mechanisms, software would carry out each instruction in precisely the same sequence regardless of shifting conditions. Programs can assess data and choose among different courses of action based on logical conditions using conditional statements. For instance, e-commerce systems check product availability before confirming an order, while banking software assesses whether sufficient funds are available before authorizing a withdrawal. These logical choices give software flexibility, intelligence, and the ability to manage a variety of scenarios that arise during regular operation.

Programs can execute the same set of instructions again without needless code duplication thanks to repetition, which is typically achieved using loops. Processing data sets, repeating computations, and continuously observing shifting circumstances are all common computational activities. Loops reduce program size and improve maintainability while providing an effective way to manage repetitive tasks. Repetition enables software to do a lot of work using clear, structured reasoning, whether it is showing a list of products, analyzing thousands of records, or doing scientific simulations. Writing excellent programs greatly benefits from knowing when and how to use loops.

By breaking complex programs into smaller, reusable parts, functions embody modular programming. Developers group similar processes into distinct functions that carry out particular duties rather than putting every instruction in a single sequence. This modular approach enhances readability, simplifies debugging, promotes code reuse, and facilitates multi-developer collaboration. By enabling programmers to concentrate on the results of a specific operation without constantly thinking about its internal implementation, functions also encourage abstraction. To provide extensive functionality while maintaining manageable organization, large software systems may include hundreds or thousands of functions operating simultaneously.

Software is connected to people and external systems through input and output processes. The data that programs receive from keyboards, touchscreens, files, sensors, databases, or network connections is referred to as input. The findings displayed on screens, printed on paper, delivered via speakers, stored in files, or transmitted over communication networks are referred to as output. Because users may offer unexpected or inaccurate information, proper management of input and output is necessary for effective programming. As a result, programs should check input, gracefully manage mistakes, and generate output that is understandable to users. Software quality and user satisfaction are greatly affected by reliable input and output processing.

Debugging is an essential skill closely related to programming logic. Because large systems require many interacting components and logical decisions, errors are unavoidable throughout software development. Debugging entails finding, evaluating, and fixing these mistakes by methodical research. Expert programmers look at program behavior, trace execution pathways, evaluate variable values, and identify the source of faulty results rather than speculating about potential causes. This methodical approach emphasizes the value of logical reasoning while strengthening analytical thinking. Every debugging experience enhances future problem-solving skills and broadens comprehension of programming ideas.

By confirming that software functions properly in a variety of scenarios, testing supports troubleshooting. When given new data or uncommon situations, a program that works well for one input may abruptly fail. To ensure consistent reliability, extensive testing covers typical usage, boundary conditions, invalid inputs, and extreme circumstances. Programmers must consider how users might interact with software and anticipate potential issues before they arise to conduct effective testing. This proactive approach helps create reliable apps that continue to operate as needs change.

Another crucial factor in programming logic is efficiency. While an accurate answer is important, programmers also aim to create solutions that run fast, use little memory, and scale well as data volumes rise. Choosing the right algorithms, carefully arranging data, and eliminating pointless operations are all common components of efficient programming. Efficiency gains can significantly affect application performance, especially in systems that analyze large datasets or handle millions of transactions. Developers are encouraged to assess various strategies and select solutions that strike a balance between speed, resource utilization, readability, and maintainability when they have an understanding of efficiency.

Because software development is sometimes a team endeavor, readability is equally crucial. Months or years after they are first created, programs should make their purpose evident to both the original author and other developers. While lowering maintenance costs, logical arrangement, meaningful variable names, descriptive function names, and consistent formatting enhance comprehension. Clear programming logic facilitates debugging, fosters collaboration, and allows for future improvements without adding needless complexity. Professionalism and thorough attention to long-term software quality are demonstrated by readable code.

Additionally, programming logic promotes abstraction, enabling developers to hide unnecessary complexity and focus on key concepts. The numerous interrelated parts, libraries, and frameworks that make up modern software systems simplify development by providing reusable functionality. To use these components efficiently, programmers do not need to understand every internal detail. Rather, they rely on clear interfaces that specify how the components should be used. Large-scale software development is made possible by abstraction, which lessens cognitive load and frees developers to focus on higher-level issues.

Rather than relying solely on memorization, learning programming logic involves regular practice. Genuine comprehension is developed through writing programs, problem-solving, experimenting with new approaches, and reflecting on mistakes. However, reading books and examining examples provide essential theoretical knowledge. Every programming project presents new challenges that enhance logical thinking and expand conceptual understanding. Over time, students acquire the intuition necessary to identify patterns, create algorithms, and choose the best course of action in progressively challenging circumstances. This steady advancement strengthens self-assurance while reiterating timeless ideas relevant to evolving technologies.

Ultimately, the intellectual basis for all software development lies in understanding programming logic and fundamental concepts. These concepts enable students to adapt successfully throughout their careers, regardless of specific programming languages or technological developments. Aspiring programmers can turn concepts into dependable, efficient software solutions by learning algorithms, variables, data types, expressions, decision-making, repetition, functions, debugging, testing, efficiency, readability, and abstraction. These fundamental ideas endure as technology advances, serving as crucial tools for problem-solving, developing novel applications, and making significant contributions to the ever-growing field of computer science.

Working with Variables, Data Types, and Control Structures

One of the most basic parts of programming is working with variables, data types, and control structures, as these concepts form the foundation for developing software that is efficient, well-organized, and functional. The ability to store information, represent various types of data, and make decisions depending on changing situations is essential for any computer program, regardless of its size or complexity. Programmers can write code that is dependable, maintainable, and capable of solving real-world problems by understanding how these components interact. The fundamentals of variables, data types, and control structures are the same in almost all contemporary programming environments, despite variations in syntax and sophisticated features. Gaining proficiency in these areas provides a solid basis for understanding more complex subjects like database administration, software engineering, object-oriented programming, and artificial intelligence.

Programs can retain and modify data while operating thanks to variables, which serve as temporary storage. Programmers use variables to store data that may change while a program is running, just as humans use labeled containers to organize various goods. The code is made easier to read and comprehend by giving each variable a meaningful name that clarifies its function. A variable could hold a customer's name, a product's price, a student's exam result, or the temperature as provided by a sensor. Instead of entering the same data repeatedly throughout a program, developers store it in variables so it can be accessed, modified, and reused as needed. This method reduces errors caused by repetitive coding while increasing efficiency.

Declaring a variable's name and defining the kind of data it will hold are often steps in the creation process. While some programming languages automatically determine the type based on the supplied value, others need developers to explicitly define the data type of the variable before it can be used. Careful variable naming is still a crucial programming technique, regardless of the language. In addition to helping other developers comprehend the logic of the software without requiring lengthy explanations, descriptive names convey the purpose of stored information. Vague labels like value1 or data2 are far less informative than meaningful names like customer Balance, total Sales, or student Age. Clear naming standards greatly enhance software readability and long-term maintainability.

Information that changes while a program is running can be stored in variables. For instance, when clients add or remove items from their shopping carts, an online shopping program updates the total purchase amount continuously. In a similar vein, a game may use variables that change often during gameplay to store a player's score, remaining lives, and current position. Variables serve as the basis for dynamic software that can respond to user input and real-world events because they enable programs to monitor changing conditions. Programs would be restricted to constant values rather than variables, making it impossible for them to perform useful calculations or adapt to changing circumstances.

Data types, which specify the type of information a variable can store, are closely related to variables. Data types enable accurate interpretation and processing of information by computers. Data types offer significant distinctions that direct computations, comparisons, and storage techniques because computers internally encode all information as binary values. Program performance, accuracy, and efficiency can all be enhanced by choosing the right data type. Avoiding incompatible actions that might lead to inaccurate outcomes or unexpected behavior also reduces programming errors.

The integer data type, which represents whole numbers without decimal points, is one of the most widely used. For counting objects, maintaining ages, keeping track of inventory amounts, computing scores, or representing identification numbers, integers are perfect. Integers are commonly used in software development because they support efficient arithmetic operations and require comparatively little memory. However, integers are inappropriate for applications involving measurements, financial computations, or scientific data that require decimal precision, since they cannot effectively represent fractional quantities.

Decimal values can be represented as floating-point numbers. Calculations involving fractions, percentages, lengths, temperatures, and several scientific measurements are supported by these data types. Floating-point calculations play a major role in financial software, engineering simulations, weather forecasting systems, and graphical applications. Programmers must be aware of the limits of floating-point numbers, even if they significantly increase computational power. Tiny rounding mistakes can happen during computations because computers internally approximate a lot of decimal values. These errors can be reduced with careful programming techniques, particularly in applications that demand high numerical precision.

Individual symbols, including letters, numerals, punctuation, and special characters, are stored in character data types. Characters are frequently used to represent encoded data, computer commands, user input, and page contents. Strings, which stand for entire words, sentences, or longer text blocks, can be created by combining many letters. Since almost all applications process textual data, strings are essential to modern software. String manipulation is widely used in email systems, search engines, messaging platforms, websites, databases, and document editors. Strings can be efficiently compared, combined, searched, modified, and analyzed thanks to the specialized operations that programming languages usually offer.

One of the most basic yet effective programming concepts is the Boolean data type. There are just two potential values for a Boolean variable, which are often represented as true or false. Boolean values allow software to regulate program behavior and make logical conclusions, despite their seeming simplicity. Conditions, including whether a user has supplied a valid password, whether there is sufficient inventory for a purchase, or whether uploaded material meets standards, are commonly assessed by programs. The Boolean results of these evaluations determine the software's next course of action. Boolean logic is used widely in almost all current applications to create intelligent, responsive behavior.

Several programming languages also support more complex data structures that group related values. Developers can effectively handle collections of data by using arrays, lists, dictionaries, and objects. These complex structures show how basic principles come together to enable progressively more complex applications, even as they build on the fundamental ideas of variables and data types. Later in their programming journey, learners may work confidently with these larger organizational structures if they have a solid understanding of fundamental data types.

The sequence in which program instructions are carried out is determined by control structures. Without control structures, computers couldn't adjust to changing circumstances; they would process instructions sequentially from start to finish. By enabling software to make choices, repeat tasks, and logically arrange execution, control structures add flexibility. These features turn straightforward instruction sequences into dynamic programs that can manage challenging real-world situations. Control structures are necessary for any interactive application to react correctly to changes in the environment and user activities.

Programming's default control structure is sequential execution. Instructions are processed one after another in the order they occur during sequential execution. This simple method is effective for activities like reading data, performing calculations, and displaying outcomes that require a set of processing stages. Sequential execution, despite its simplicity, is the foundation of all programs, as it underpins all other control structures. Programmers can better organize code and identify opportunities to add more complex decision-making or repetition by having a solid understanding of sequential logic.

Programs can choose among different courses of action based on predetermined criteria, thanks to selection structures. Selection statements assess logical expressions and only run the relevant code, as opposed to executing all instructions without any conditions. For instance, an online banking system verifies whether there are enough funds before authorizing a withdrawal. In contrast, an educational application uses computed scores to assess whether a student has completed an exam. These decision-making skills enable software to effectively adjust to changing circumstances, enhancing user experience and functionality. Numerous nested decisions that cooperate to address a variety of operational conditions are frequently seen in complex applications.

Logical operators and comparison play a major role in the conditions utilized in selection structures. Relationships among values, such as equality, inequality, or numerical ordering, are determined using comparison operators. Logical operators combine multiple conditions to produce more complex decision-making procedures. For instance, before allowing account access, software can demand both a valid security code and a correct password. Programmers can create precise decision-making logic and prevent inadvertent behavior caused by incorrect expressions or operator precedence by understanding how conditions are evaluated.

Programs can execute the same instructions repeatedly without needlessly duplicating code thanks to repetition structures, also known as loops. Processing massive amounts of data, repeating computations, monitoring system activities, and waiting for user input are all common computational tasks. By automatically repeating certain instructions until predetermined conditions are met, loops offer an effective solution. While a search engine uses repeated operations to process millions of documents, a payroll system can use a loop to calculate compensation for hundreds of employees. Repetition structures improve maintainability and execution performance while significantly reducing code length.

Different looping techniques support different programming scenarios. Certain loops are appropriate for jobs with unpredictable completion times because they keep running as long as certain requirements are met. Others provide effective methods when the required number of iterations is known, such as repeating instructions a set number of times. Regardless of the particular looping mechanism employed, proper design avoids typical programming mistakes like infinite loops, in which execution never ends because terminating criteria are never met. Thus, knowing loop behavior helps ensure that software is correct and that resources are used effectively.

Throughout a program's execution, variables, data types, and control structures work together continuously. Control structures dictate how the program reacts to changing values, variables store information, and data types specify how that information should be processed. For instance, a weather monitoring program uses loops to periodically evaluate incoming sensor data, stores temperature measurements in floating-point variables, and compares those values using Boolean conditions. In a similar vein, an online exam system records student answers, assesses scores, uses conditional statements to generate pass-or-fail results, and repeats the grading process for numerous participants. These interwoven interactions show how basic programming ideas come together to create useful software behavior.

The correct usage of variables, data types, and control structures is also crucial to error prevention. Software errors are often caused by poorly designed decision logic, improper data type selection, or incorrect variable initialization. To ensure that variables contain accurate data, operations adhere to data type restrictions, and control structures function as intended, programmers use meticulous planning, testing, and debugging procedures. To help developers find issues before users use the software, modern programming languages often include tools that automatically detect specific types of errors. However, since automated technologies cannot replace careful program design, solid conceptual knowledge is still necessary.

Effective organization of variables and control structures becomes more crucial as software systems grow in size and complexity. A clear program organization enhances readability, makes debugging easier, and facilitates multi-developer collaboration. Software quality can be sustained over time through well-organized control flow, logical grouping of relevant variables, and consistent naming conventions. Future changes are made possible by these procedures without adding needless complexity or unforeseen consequences. Therefore, professional software engineering prioritizes code clarity and long-term maintainability in addition to functional correctness.

The fundamental basis of all programming ultimately lies in variables, data types, and control structures. These ideas enable computers to carry out repetitive operations efficiently, store information, represent many types of data, and make intelligent decisions. These fundamental ideas are remarkably consistent across various technologies and development environments, even as programming languages constantly change. By grasping variables, understanding appropriate data types, and creating efficient control structures, students gain the logical abilities required to develop reliable software, solve more complex problems, and confidently transition into more advanced computer science fields. These core notions serve as a link between theoretical knowledge and practical software development, enabling programmers to translate concepts into useful programs that meet real-world demands precisely, effectively, and creatively.

Mastering Functions, Modular Design, and Code Organization

To become a proficient programmer and software developer, one must grasp functionalities, modular design, and code organization. An organized approach to writing code is necessary to create larger and more dependable applications, whereas beginners frequently concentrate on learning programming grammar and solving basic problems. Maintaining a single block of instructions becomes harder as software projects grow larger and more complex. Unorganized programs are more difficult to comprehend, debug, alter, and grow. By pushing programmers to break down complex systems into smaller, more manageable components, functions, and modular designs, these approaches offer solutions to these problems. These guidelines facilitate cooperation, make maintenance easier, enhance readability, and allow software to change effectively over time.

A function is a standalone chunk of code that is intended to carry out a particular purpose. Programmers put the same instructions inside a function that can be called whenever necessary rather than duplicating them throughout a program. This method reduces needless duplication while improving the clarity and conciseness of programs. An online shopping application might, for instance, compute taxes, verify user input, or generate multiple receipts while it is running. Instead of continually writing the same code, developers write separate functions that perform each of these tasks. To ensure consistency and minimize development effort, the application calls the relevant function whenever the feature is needed.

One of the most important ideas in software development is reusability, which is supported by functions. Because engineers don't have to redo pre-existing solutions each time a similar problem arises, reusable code saves time. Well-designed functions can frequently be used with little to no modification across several projects. Functions that verify email addresses, compute discounts, format dates, or handle payments, for instance, may have a wide range of uses across various sectors. Because thoroughly tested routines are less likely to have faults when reused in future projects, reusability not only speeds up software development but also increases dependability.

Enhanced readability is a key advantage of functions. Even seasoned programmers find it difficult to understand large programs with thousands of consecutive instructions. Programs can be broken down into clearly named functions so that readers can grasp the overall structure without having to examine every implementation detail immediately. A long series of mathematical operations placed directly within the main program is far less effective at communicating its goal than a function called calculate Monthly Payment. Descriptive function names serve as documentation, which speeds up programmers' understanding of software behavior and greatly simplifies maintenance throughout a project.

The practice of concealing superfluous complexity while revealing only necessary functionality is known as abstraction, and functions play a part in this process. Programmers frequently need to know what a function does when utilizing it, not how it carries out its internal processes. Developers may concentrate on resolving more complex issues without becoming sidetracked by implementation specifics because of this division. For example, when a software system invokes a function to encrypt sensitive data, the programmer doesn't need to verify every internal mathematical calculation because they can trust that the function will encrypt the data correctly. As a result, abstraction reduces cognitive complexity and enables software systems to scale without becoming uncontrollable.

Functions can receive data through parameters in most programming languages. As input values, parameters provide the information needed for a function to perform its operation. Because the same logic can process new data each time it is called, this feature gives functions considerable flexibility. For instance, a function that computes a rectangle's area can accommodate various width and height values without requiring several iterations of the same code. Parameterized functions become more flexible, reusable, and simpler to maintain as requirements shift by separating logic from specific data.

Additionally, a lot of functions generate return values that give the calling application the results. These functions compute data and return the result for additional processing rather than just carrying out an operation. A function might compute the total cost of an online purchase, determine whether a password satisfies security criteria, or return a student's final grade. By combining several functions, returning values allows programs to create progressively complex operations. Because the output of one function often becomes the input of another, complex systems can arise from straightforward, well-defined building blocks that logically interact with one another.

By dividing entire software systems into separate parts, known as modules, modular design builds on the concept of functions. A module is a collection of related variables, functions, and resources that share a common objective.

Developers divide functionality into useful pieces rather than putting every feature in one big file. An online banking system might, for instance, have distinct modules for account transactions, client management, reporting, security, and authentication. Through well-created well-designed interfaces, each module interacts with other modules while focusing on a particular task. Because programmers can work on particular modules without having to comprehend every facet of the entire system at once, this organization makes development easier.

Supporting maintainability is one of the biggest advantages of modular design. When businesses add new features, enhance performance, or respond to user input, software requirements often shift. Programs constructed according to modular principles are better able to adapt to these changes because they remain contained within specific components. Developers generally alter the payment module when a business updates its payment processing system, leaving unrelated components of the program unaffected. This isolation shortens the development time for upcoming improvements and lowers the possibility of introducing inadvertent errors.

Additionally, modular architecture facilitates cooperation between development teams. Dozens or perhaps hundreds of programmers collaborate on modern software projects. It would be quite challenging to coordinate these efforts without prior planning. Modules minimize conflict by enabling team members to assign tasks based on expertise. Networking functions might be developed by one group, database operations by another, and security or user interface design by still others. Throughout the software lifecycle, concurrent development, effective testing, and more seamless project management are made possible by clearly defined module boundaries.

Improved testing is a major benefit of modular architecture. It can be difficult to verify the accuracy of a complete application at once, particularly for huge systems with millions of lines of code. Developers can test individual components separately before incorporating them into the entire application, thanks to modular architecture. Every module is thoroughly tested to make sure it functions properly in a variety of scenarios. Errors are contained within smaller parts rather than concealed among thousands of unrelated instructions, making problem identification considerably easier. This methodical testing procedure greatly enhances software dependability and overall product quality.

The deliberate placement of software components to enhance readability, maintainability, and long-term usability is referred to as code organization. Consistent structures, naming standards, formatting styles, and documentation techniques are all part of well-organized code. Software can be written in a variety of ways through programming languages, but disciplined organization enables developers to comprehend and confidently modify programs swiftly. Software that remains usable years after its development is made possible by standardized file structures, logical grouping of similar functions, consistent indentation, and relevant comments.

To organize code effectively, naming conventions are crucial. Names for variables, functions, classes, and modules should be descriptive and clearly convey their purpose. Meaningful names minimize the need for superfluous remarks while reducing confusion. A function named calculate Employee Salary, for instance, clearly communicates its goal right away, but a name as ambiguous as process Data provides no helpful information. In a similar vein, generic labels like value1 or variable X are less clear than variables like customer Name or account Balance. Because programmers can comprehend new code more quickly, good naming standards enhance teamwork.

By displaying code in an orderly and predictable way, consistent formatting improves readability even further. Nested control structures are visually distinguished by indentation, which facilitates the recognition of logical links. Standardized spacing enhances visual clarity, while blank lines divide similar code sections. To ensure uniformity across large projects, many development teams set formatting standards that all members must adhere to. Although formatting decisions have little effect on program execution, they have a big impact on how simple it is for humans to comprehend, review, and maintain software.

By elucidating ideas that might not be immediately apparent from the implementation itself, documentation enhances well-organized code. Although descriptive names eliminate the need for lengthy comments, some algorithms, design choices, or technical limitations may require more justification. Good documentation makes it easier for future developers to understand the rationale behind specific strategies and the interactions among components. However, excessive or outdated comments can lead to confusion; thus, documentation should remain precise, succinct, and focused on information that is not already clear from well-written code.

Another key component of modular software design is the separation of concerns. Instead of trying to complete several unrelated tasks, each function or module should focus on one clearly stated duty. For instance, a function that verifies user input shouldn't compute financial totals or provide reports. Testing, debugging, and future change are made easier by restricting each component to a single function. Developers can enhance one part of the product without inadvertently impacting others when duties are kept distinct. This methodical approach greatly enhances the quality and maintainability of software.

The continuous process of improving code organization without altering the product's external behavior is known as refactoring. Opportunities to streamline operations, remove duplication, enhance nomenclature, or rearrange modules frequently arise as programmers gain expertise or project needs change. Refactoring preserves current functionality while fortifying program architecture. Throughout the development process, skilled developers frequently improve code rather than waiting until projects become challenging to maintain. Technical debt, which occurs when disorganized code accumulates and eventually hampers future progress, can be avoided through continuous improvement.

The significance of reusable libraries and frameworks, which extend modular design concepts beyond individual projects, is also emphasized in modern software development. Libraries include sets of tried-and-true routines that address typical programming problems, including database access, networking, graphical user interfaces, and mathematical computations. Frameworks provide structured structures that use pre-established design patterns to arrange complete programs. By using these reusable components, developers can leverage community-tested reliability and ongoing improvements without having to start from scratch.

Scalability is also supported by well-organized code, which enables programs to expand without becoming unmanageable. While commercial apps frequently include thousands of interrelated components built over many years, small educational programs might have a few features. This expansion is made possible by modular structures, which maintain a clear structure even as complexity rises. Teams can grow without interfering with established development procedures, new features may be added through extra modules, and current components can be upgraded or replaced separately. Therefore, careful software design is just as important to scalability as hardware resources.

In the end, learning functions, modular architecture, and code organization gives programmers the tools they need to create dependable, manageable, and high-caliber software. These ideas turn disjointed programming instructions into coherent systems that are simpler to comprehend, test, alter, and grow. Modular design breaks down complicated applications into smaller parts, functions encourage reuse and abstraction, and well-organized code guarantees long-term readability and cooperation. When combined, these ideas provide the architectural foundation for contemporary software engineering, enabling programmers to design systems that continue to function well as technology advances and user needs change. Early adoption of these techniques helps students create lifelong success in computer science and software development.

Developing Effective Debugging and Testing Habits

One of the most crucial abilities in programming and software development is establishing efficient testing and debugging routines. Creating dependable software involves more than just writing code. Finding any issues that prevent the software from operating properly and confirming that it behaves as planned under a variety of circumstances are equally crucial. Because software systems sometimes comprise thousands or even millions of interacting instructions, even skilled programmers rarely write perfect code on their first try. Programs may fail or generate inaccurate results due to small errors, missed assumptions, or unanticipated user behavior. Before software is used by people, debugging and testing offer organized ways to find, comprehend, and fix these problems. Programmers enhance the quality of their software, hone their problem-solving skills, and boost their self-confidence by forming disciplined habits in these areas.

The methodical process of finding, examining, and fixing mistakes in a computer program is called debugging. Effective debugging depends on thorough observation and rational investigation rather than only speculating about what might be wrong. Debugging is the process of identifying the root cause of a programming error by collecting evidence and analyzing the program's behavior while it runs. Successful programmers can be distinguished from those who grow discouraged by constant trial and error using this analytical method. Skilled developers follow a rigorous process that enables them to identify issues and effectively fix them rather than making haphazard modifications to the code.

Programming errors typically fall into several broad types, each of which calls for a unique method of rectification. Code that deviates from a programming language's grammatical rules is called a syntax error. Compilers and interpreters typically identify these issues automatically before the program starts. Syntax problems are frequently caused by missing punctuation, misspelled terms, mismatched brackets, and inappropriate formatting. These errors serve as a reminder to programmers of the value of meticulous attention to detail and expertise with language syntax, even if they are typically simple to fix.

Unlike compilation errors, runtime errors occur during program execution. When the application encounters unforeseen circumstances such as dividing by zero, accessing unavailable files, exceeding memory constraints, or attempting invalid operations, these errors occur. If runtime errors are not handled correctly, the program may abruptly terminate or exhibit unpredictable behavior. By validating input, verifying resource availability, and implementing error-handling mechanisms that enable software to recover gracefully wherever possible, skilled programmers anticipate many of these scenarios.

Because the program runs without crashing yet yields inaccurate results, logic mistakes are frequently the most difficult kind of programming difficulty. A loop may process the wrong number of items, a condition may evaluate incorrectly, or a calculation may produce erroneous results. Since the software appears to operate normally, it is necessary to carefully examine the underlying logic to pinpoint the source of the improper behavior. Because programmers must compare the program's anticipated behavior with its actual behavior and identify where the reasoning deviates from expectations, solving logic errors improves computational thinking.

Creating a methodical debugging procedure significantly increases productivity and lowers frustration. Reproducing the issue regularly is the first step. Finding the cause of an error becomes much more challenging if it occurs infrequently or under unknown circumstances. Programmers establish a trustworthy environment for research by pinpointing the precise series of events that cause the issue. Information about the program's behavior before, during, and after the error is collected once the issue can be consistently reproduced. This methodical technique helps developers focus on relevant evidence and avoid wasted effort.

One of the simplest yet most useful debugging techniques is to study error messages carefully. When programs run across issues, modern programming environments offer comprehensive information. Error messages frequently pinpoint the problem's location, explain its nature, and offer potential solutions. While seasoned programmers see these signals as useful diagnostic tools, beginners occasionally disregard them or see them as baffling roadblocks. Debugging is greatly accelerated, and programming concepts are better understood when one learns to read compiler errors, runtime exceptions, and warning messages.

Effective debugging is further supported by segmenting big problems into smaller parts. Because there are numerous interdependent components in complex software systems, it can be challenging to identify which part is responsible for the inappropriate behavior. Programmers reduce the scope of their search and streamline analysis by isolating specific functions, modules, or code segments. Testing a single component at a time simplifies the process and makes it easier to determine whether issues stem from interactions among components or from a particular function. The more general problem-solving techniques applied in computer science are reflected in this divide-and-conquer tactic.

Another useful debugging method is to trace program execution. While monitoring how variables change throughout execution, programmers follow the computer's instructions. It is frequently possible to identify the initial instances of inaccurate calculations, unforeseen circumstances, or inadvertent choices by looking at intermediate numbers. Debugging tools that let developers halt execution, examine variable contents, carry out commands step-by-step, and interactively monitor program flow are found in many integrated development environments. These features turn debugging from a haphazard approach into a methodical investigation backed by concrete proof.

Even with the advent of sophisticated development tools, printing diagnostic data is still a useful debugging technique. Programmers can learn more about how software operates internally by temporarily displaying variable values, execution paths, or intermediate calculations. These diagnostic statements help confirm assumptions and highlight differences between the program's behavior and expectations. Temporary diagnostic output offers a straightforward and efficient way to understand complex execution sequences during development, though it should usually be removed before software launch.

Debugging requires perseverance and patience because complex issues rarely show up right away. Complex software systems frequently have several interrelated problems, and fixing one mistake could reveal another that was previously undetected. Successful programmers acknowledge this fact and tackle debugging with resolve rather than annoyance. Every problem that is fixed advances knowledge of the program and the fundamental concepts of programming. Repetitive debugging experiences improve analytical thinking, attention to detail, and confidence in resolving progressively difficult technical issues over time.

By confirming that software meets its intended criteria in a variety of scenarios, testing enhances debugging. Testing seeks to identify issues before users experience them, whereas debugging focuses on fixing them. Effective testing assesses how software responds to uncommon inputs, unforeseen circumstances, and boundary conditions, in addition to determining whether it operates successfully under typical circumstances. Extensive testing reduces the likelihood of costly failures after deployment, boosts user confidence, and enhances reliability.

Verifying software with realistic input values is a crucial testing principle. When consumers submit partial, inaccurate, or unexpected data, programs frequently behave appropriately. As a result, testing involves examining typical scenarios as well as invalid inputs, excessively large or small values, empty fields, special characters, and unusual data combinations. Programmers find flaws in software that might go unreported until deployment by considering how actual users might interact with it.

Because errors often arise near the boundaries of permissible input ranges, boundary testing is another important practice. For instance, software might work properly for ages ranging from eighteen to sixty-five, but it might not work at precisely eighteen, precisely sixty-five, or at numbers just outside those ranges. Array sizes, financial computations, dates, percentages, and a plethora of other programming contexts all have comparable boundary constraints. It is possible to find subtle logic flaws that regular testing might miss by carefully checking these crucial numbers.

By confirming functionality as new features are added rather than waiting until an application is finished, incremental testing promotes effective software development. Immediately upon implementation, small portions of the code are tested, allowing issues to be found while they are still relatively straightforward. Because recent changes are easier to review than changes accumulated over several weeks or months, this approach makes it easier to find newly introduced problems. Additionally, incremental testing promotes ongoing development process improvement.

In contemporary software engineering, automated testing has grown in significance. Every time software is modified, developers create automated tests that execute predefined scenarios rather than manually repeating the same verification steps. These tests identify unforeseen side effects created during development while confirming that current functionality continues to perform as planned. Large development teams can maintain software quality despite frequent upgrades thanks to automated testing, which also saves time and increases consistency. Even though developing automated tests takes more work at first, the long-term advantages far exceed the cost.

The specific goal of regression testing is to ensure that features that were previously functional continue to function after changes are made. As software develops, adding new features often causes unanticipated disruptions to current behavior. Regression testing continually examines previous features to ensure that enhancements haven't introduced new flaws elsewhere in the system. This approach is especially helpful for big projects when several developers make simultaneous changes to related components. Regression testing should be done consistently to maintain software stability over time.

Effective testing and debugging practices are also greatly aided by documentation. Important references for future development are created by documenting problems, their causes, the remedies implemented, and the lessons learned. Development teams can identify recurring trends, avoid making the same mistakes twice, and fix similar difficulties faster when issues are well-documented. By allowing team members to exchange information about program behavior, testing protocols, and known constraints, documentation also promotes collaboration. Thus, keeping correct records improves corporate effectiveness as well as individual learning.

By keeping track of past code modifications, version control systems improve debugging even further. Programmers can compare the present code with previous iterations to determine precisely what changed when new issues arise following recent changes. This feature makes research easier and lowers the possibility of losing earlier work while conducting experiments. By monitoring the contributions of several team members and offering methods for securely incorporating new features into ongoing projects, version control also promotes collaborative development.

Debugging and testing become routine programming practices when one adopts a continuous improvement attitude. Experienced developers see mistakes as chances to deepen expertise and enhance software quality rather than as failures. Each identified flaw provides important details about user expectations, program behavior, or design assumptions. Rather than discouraging, this optimistic viewpoint promotes thorough investigation, deliberate testing, and continuous improvement. Cleaner designs and more dependable implementations are the result of programmers' growing ability to anticipate such issues before they arise.

Because various people frequently see problems that others miss, collaboration increases the efficacy of debugging and testing. Software is exposed to several viewpoints through code reviews, pair programming, and team conversations, increasing the likelihood of finding hidden issues. One's own understanding is often clarified, and presumptions that may need reexamination are revealed when one explains program logic to coworkers. While encouraging uniform quality standards throughout development teams, constructive criticism promotes learning. Thus, individual analytical abilities, team evaluation, and shared accountability for quality are all necessary for successful software engineering.

In the end, creating dependable, manageable, and expert software requires developing efficient debugging and testing practices. While testing confirms that applications operate successfully in a variety of scenarios, debugging enhances logical reasoning by promoting methodical analysis of code faults. When combined, these methods raise user satisfaction, lower maintenance costs, and enhance software quality. More significantly, they foster traits that go well beyond programming itself, such as patience, analytical thinking, attention to detail, and ongoing learning. Disciplined testing and debugging practices remain essential tools for developing reliable technology that users can confidently rely on as software systems grow more complex and integrated into every facet of contemporary life.

CHAPTER III
Exploring Essential Computer Science Disciplines

Understanding Data Structures and Algorithms

Since data structures and algorithms are the cornerstones of effective software development, comprehending them is one of the most significant learning milestones in computer science. Programming languages provide the means to write code, but data structures and algorithms determine how effectively that code addresses problems. Even if a program produces the correct result, it may be useless in the real world if it takes too long or uses too much memory. Developers must carefully organize data and design logical processes that optimize efficiency while preserving reliability as software systems continue to grow in size and complexity. Programmers can design programs that are not only functional but also efficient, scalable, and capable of handling more complex computing tasks by mastering data structures and algorithms.

A data structure is a systematic approach to managing, storing, and organizing data so that it can be effectively accessed and modified. Every day, computers handle massive volumes of data, including financial transactions, medical histories, customer records, scientific measurements, multimedia content, and a wide range of other digital data types. Retrieval and processing would be incredibly slow and ineffective if this data were just stored in an unorganized manner. Data structures offer thoughtfully crafted ways to organize information in accordance with the particular requirements of various applications. Programmers can increase software performance, streamline development, and use fewer resources by choosing the right structure.

By providing the algorithms needed to handle ordered data, algorithms serve as a complement to data structures. An algorithm is a precise set of instructions that completes a task or solves a specific problem. Algorithms are the foundation of every computer program, whether it is used for alphabetical name sorting, information retrieval, financial report computation, file compression, sensitive data encryption, or online product recommendations. Algorithms specify both what a program does and how effectively it accomplishes its goals. Algorithm design is one of the core fields of computer science because a well-designed algorithm frequently completes the same work far more quickly than a less effective option.

Algorithms and data structures are closely linked. While the usefulness of a data structure often depends on the algorithms that operate on it, a well-designed algorithm requires an appropriate data structure to achieve optimal performance. Even if the program is still conceptually valid, selecting the incorrect combination might drastically degrade software efficiency. For instance, different organizational strategies are needed for an application that regularly searches vast amounts of data than for one that is primarily concerned with creating new records. Instead of relying on a single, all-encompassing strategy, programmers can make well-informed design decisions tailored to each project's specific requirements by understanding this relationship.

The array, which keeps several items of the same type at successive memory regions, is one of the most basic data structures. Because each position can be easily determined using its index, arrays offer quick access to individual elements. Because of this feature, arrays are very effective in applications such as image processing, numerical analysis, and game creation that frequently need to access data by position. Arrays do have some restrictions, though. Inserting or removing values frequently necessitates changing existing elements, since they occupy fixed memory locations, reducing the efficiency of some operations. Programmers can decide when arrays are the best option by understanding both their advantages and disadvantages.

Because they allow elements to be dynamically added or removed during program execution, lists offer a more flexible way to arrange information. Lists, in contrast to arrays, don't need a set storage capacity and can expand or contract as needed. Depending on how parts are connected and accessible, different types of lists have different performance characteristics. Because of this adaptability, lists are useful for applications like customer account management, online transaction processing, and document collection organization, where the volume of data is constantly changing. Lists provide more flexibility in dynamic contexts, even if they often sacrifice some access performance compared to arrays.

Another significant data structure is a stack, which is based on the principle that the most recently added element is the first to be removed. This last-in, first-out rule is like a stack of books: you have to take out the top book before you can reach the books below. Numerous computing processes are supported by stacks, such as navigating browser history, analyzing mathematical formulas, handling function calls during program execution, and supporting undo actions in text editors. They are quite effective for issues that inherently involve nested or sequential processing because of their straightforward operational paradigm.

Queues use the first-in, first-out principle to arrange data. The earliest element added to the queue is processed first, just like people standing in line. Operating systems, network communication, printer control, task scheduling, and customer support apps all depend on queues. Queues offer a structured and effective solution where requests must be processed in the order they arrive. Queue variations also facilitate specialized applications that need circular data management or priority-based processing.

By organizing data into parent-child relationships, trees establish hierarchical organization. Trees, unlike linear structures like arrays or lists, allow data to branch into multiple levels, making them effective for representing file systems, familial relationships, organizational charts, and decision-making processes. In particular, search trees facilitate quick information retrieval by arranging items according to logical ordering criteria. Because tree structures balance effective searching, insertion, and deletion operations even while maintaining incredibly enormous datasets, many databases, search engines, and operating systems heavily rely on them.

Because they show the links between related elements, graphs offer one of the most flexible data structures. A graph consists of nodes connected by links that represent different kinds of relationships. Graph structures are widely used in social media networks, transportation systems, communication networks, recommendation systems, and mapping applications. Complex issues, including finding the shortest travel routes, discovering connected communities, optimizing delivery schedules, and examining communication patterns, are all resolved by algorithms that operate on graphs. As a result, graph theory is important in many contemporary computer applications.

Depending on the problems they are intended to tackle, algorithms differ greatly. Searching algorithms ascertain whether a particular piece of information is present in a collection and, if so, pinpoint its location. Until the required value is found or the collection is complete, linear search examines each element one at a time. Despite being simple, this approach becomes less effective as the amount of data increases. More sophisticated methods leverage structured data to reduce search times significantly. The structure of the underlying data and the frequency of queries inside the application play a major role in choosing the right searching algorithm.

Sorting algorithms arrange data in a way that makes sense, such as alphabetizing names, ranking test results, or classifying goods by cost. In many software systems, searching, reporting, and analysis are made easier by well-organized data. There are several sorting algorithms available, and depending on the dataset's size and structure, each offers distinct performance characteristics. While some work well with tiny collections, others do exceptionally well while handling millions of records. Instead of using the same approach everywhere, programmers can select solutions that best fit the needs of specific applications by being aware of these variations.

One of the key issues in computer science is algorithm efficiency. Even when two algorithms need significantly different amounts of memory or processing time, they may yield similar results. These variations grow in importance as data volumes rise. When processing one million records, an algorithm that performs satisfactorily with 100 records could become unfeasible. Therefore, computer scientists use mathematical models that predict how resource requirements increase with increasing input size to examine algorithm performance. Even while novices don't have to learn complex mathematical language right away, understanding the value of efficiency promotes careful software design from the start.

Another crucial component of algorithm analysis is memory use. While some algorithms process information more slowly and require less storage, others run quickly yet use a lot of memory. Software developers frequently balance these conflicting factors in accordance with project specifications. While scientific simulations on powerful servers might focus on processing speed, mobile applications with constrained hardware resources might prioritize memory conservation. Instead of assuming a single best course of action, developers can design solutions suited to specific operating conditions by being aware of these trade-offs.

Another important algorithmic method is recursion, in which a function solves a problem by repeatedly calling itself on smaller instances of the original problem. Elegant techniques for handling hierarchical data structures, performing mathematical operations, or exploring intricate search spaces are often provided by recursive solutions. Recursion, however, also needs to be carefully designed to prevent indefinite repetition or excessive memory usage. Programmers can solve more problems and get a deeper understanding of computing processes by learning when recursive approaches are superior to iterative ones.

Rather than depending only on familiarity or convenience, selecting the right data structures and algorithms requires a detailed analysis of the situation. When choosing implementation options, developers consider factors such as data size, update frequency, search requirements, available memory, anticipated growth, and system performance goals. One of the distinctive features of computer science is the analytical decision-making process, which relies on deliberate reasoning rather than intuition to solve problems. Skilled programmers understand that devoting time to careful design frequently averts major performance problems later in the development process.

Data structures and algorithms are used practically everywhere in computing. Search engines use sophisticated indexing systems and ranking algorithms to arrange billions of webpages. By using graph algorithms on transportation networks, navigation systems determine the most efficient routes. Streaming providers use advanced data analysis methods to make movie recommendations. Healthcare businesses use well-designed information systems to keep patient records, while financial firms use optimal database structures to conduct transactions quickly. Robotics, cloud computing, cybersecurity, artificial intelligence, and scientific research all heavily rely on effective data processing and organizing.

Learning algorithms and data structures also improves more general problem-solving skills. Instead of concentrating only on memorizing particular implementations, students learn to analyze problems, assess potential solutions, and choose strategies based on logical reasoning. This kind of thinking promotes efficiency, methodical thinking, and an understanding of the connection between theoretical ideas and real-world applications. Understanding how software libraries and development frameworks arrange and process data is beneficial even for programmers who rarely use sophisticated algorithms.

Since theoretical knowledge alone rarely results in long-lasting success, practice is still necessary to understand these concepts. Through hands-on experience, comprehension is reinforced by solving programming puzzles, implementing various data structures, comparing algorithm performance, and examining real-world applications. Every project presents an opportunity to assess design decisions, pinpoint performance improvements, and recognize how effective organization affects overall software quality. Instead of depending only on memorization, students gradually acquire intuition for identifying patterns and choosing suitable methods.

In the end, understanding data structures and algorithms provides the conceptual foundation needed to develop effective, scalable, and dependable software systems. Algorithms specify the logical processes that convert data into meaningful outcomes, whereas data structures organize information to facilitate quick access and modification. When combined, they influence how well software performs in real-world scenarios with large datasets, complex interactions, and evolving user needs. Programmers can solve difficult computational problems thoughtfully and effectively by grasping these fundamental ideas, which pave the way for further education in software engineering, artificial intelligence, data science, cybersecurity, and a host of other fields that continue to influence technology.

Learning Computer Architecture and Operating Systems

Beyond building software, understanding computer architecture and operating systems is crucial to comprehending how computers work. Operating systems show how software and hardware cooperate to provide a usable computing environment, computer architecture illustrates how hardware carries out instructions, and programming teaches developers how to create applications. Every contemporary computer runs on these two pillars. Programmers may be able to write code, but may not completely comprehend how the machine processes, manages, and executes it if they lack an understanding of computer architecture and operating systems. Gaining a firm grasp of these ideas enables students to create more effective software, solve technical issues efficiently, and make well-informed choices about system design and performance enhancement.

The design, arrangement, and functionality of the physical parts that comprise a computer system are referred to as computer architecture. To carry out instructions and process data, it explains how processors, memory, storage devices, input and output hardware, and communication channels work together. Every computer, be it a desktop, laptop, smartphone, gaming console, or cloud server, adheres to architectural rules that dictate how effectively it completes calculations. Programmers can better understand why some processes run quickly while others need more processing time or system resources by grasping these concepts.

The central processing unit, or CPU, is at the heart of any computer architecture. The processor, sometimes referred to as the computer's brain, is in charge of carrying out software-provided instructions. Every program, from a basic text editor to an intricate scientific simulation, relies on the processor to perform computations, compare values, draw logical conclusions, and manage connectivity with other hardware components. Computers can perform billions of operations per second thanks to the billions of tiny transistors in modern processors, which switch electrical signals at incredibly high speeds. Despite being invisible to users, these processes are the foundation of all digital activity.

The instruction cycle is a repeating process that the processor uses to carry out its tasks. This cycle involves the CPU retrieving an instruction from memory, interpreting its meaning, performing the relevant action, and storing the result if needed. As long as the machine is running, this process keeps repeating. Multiple instruction cycles are needed for even the most basic tasks, such as adding two integers or showing a character on the screen. Because of the incredible speed at which processors execute these cycles, users can interact with sophisticated software applications with ease, giving the impression of instantaneous response.

Because memory stores both data and instructions while programs are operating, it plays an equally important function in computer architecture. RAM, or random-access memory, provides short-term storage that enables the processor to retrieve information quickly. The operating system loads instructions from permanent storage into RAM when users run an application, allowing the CPU to access them right away. RAM greatly enhances program performance since it provides far faster access than storage disks. RAM is volatile, though, so when the computer loses power, its contents are lost. This feature sets it apart from permanent storage devices that retain data even after they are shut down.

Operating systems, apps, and user files can be stored for a long time on permanent storage devices. Solid-state drives use electrical memory chips without moving elements, whereas conventional hard disk drives store data magnetically on revolving disks. Compared to conventional hard disks, solid-state drives often offer faster data access, increased durability, and reduced power consumption. All data is digitally encoded until the operating system requests it, regardless of the storage mechanism. Selected data is moved into RAM, so the CPU can access it easily when needed. A key component of computer operation is the constant flow of data between memory, storage, and the processor.

Buses are specialized channels that allow hardware components to communicate with one another. Data, memory locations, and control signals are transported across the computer system via these communication channels. Address buses locate memory locations used for processing, control buses coordinate hardware component actions, and data buses carry information between the CPU and other devices. Because information transfer delays can reduce processing efficiency even when the processor runs at very high speeds, effective communication across these buses has a substantial impact on overall system performance.

Computers can obtain information from users and the external environment through input devices. Input methods that translate physical movements or environmental conditions into digital information include keyboards, mice, touchscreens, microphones, cameras, scanners, sensors, and network connections. For the processor to understand and process external signals, each input device converts them into electrical patterns. Computers wouldn't be able to connect with humans or react to real-world events without dependable input systems.

By displaying processed data in ways that users can comprehend, output devices serve the opposite purpose. Speakers produce music, printers produce tangible documents, monitors show visual data, and specialist gadgets like virtual reality headsets offer immersive experiences. Each display, sound, or printed character is the product of considerable processing performed by the CPU, memory, and supporting hardware, even though the output appears natural to human users. Learners can better appreciate the coordinated operation of contemporary computing systems by understanding this translation of digital information into meaningful output.

Specialized processing components that improve performance for certain activities are also part of computer architecture. Highly parallel mathematical computations are carried out by graphics processing units, or GPUs, to assist artificial intelligence, video rendering, gaming, and scientific simulations. GPUs, in contrast to general-purpose processors, are made up of thousands of tiny processing units that can do multiple calculations at once. This specialized architecture significantly accelerates applications involving graphics, machine learning, and data processing. To achieve optimal performance across a variety of tasks, modern computing increasingly relies on collaboration between CPUs and GPUs.

Operating systems provide users with a convenient environment to run applications while managing all hardware operations. Programmers would have to interact directly with physical components in the absence of an operating system, significantly increasing software complexity. Rather, the operating system acts as a bridge between hardware and applications, controlling memory, organizing files, scheduling processor time, managing resources, and enabling device connectivity. Instead of managing low-level hardware processes, this abstraction enables application developers to concentrate on resolving user issues.

Process management is one of an operating system's main duties. A process is a program that the processor is currently running. Dozens or even hundreds of processes, including user applications, background services, system utilities, and security software, are frequently running concurrently on modern systems. The operating system quickly switches between processes because the processor cannot run all of them at once, allocating processor time according to meticulously crafted scheduling algorithms. This quick switching ensures effective use of computer resources while giving the impression that several programs are running at once.

Another crucial duty of operating systems is memory management. The operating system determines how memory is allocated among competing processes because RAM is limited. It protects programs from interacting with one another, allocates memory regions to applications, and retrieves unused memory when processes end. When actual RAM is insufficient, applications can use portions of storage devices as temporary memory via virtual memory, which is implemented in many operating systems. These methods allow computers to run applications larger than the available physical memory while still performing consistently.

File management provides organized techniques for storing, accessing, editing, and safeguarding digital data. To assist users in organizing documents, applications, multimedia files, and system resources, operating systems generate hierarchical directory structures. While guaranteeing effective access during regular operation, file systems preserve information about file names, locations, sizes, permissions, and modification dates. Regardless of the underlying storage technology, operating systems allow users and applications to interact with files through uniform interfaces by abstracting physical storage features.

Operating systems can coordinate interactions with many hardware components thanks to device management. Device drivers are specialized software required for each input device, output device, storage unit, and network adapter. Drivers convert basic operating system commands into instructions tailored to a device's hardware. Applications can communicate with printers, screens, keyboards, and other peripherals using this standardized method without needing in-depth knowledge of how they work inside. Thus, device management facilitates compatibility across a wide range of hardware configurations while streamlining software development.

One of the more crucial features of contemporary operating systems is security. Sensitive personal, financial, medical, and organizational data is frequently stored on computers; thus, preventing unwanted access is crucial. Operating systems employ permission systems that limit resource utilization based on user identities and security policies, access control policies, encryption support, and authentication techniques. Additionally, they keep an eye on system activity, separate apps from one another, and deliver updates that fix recently found vulnerabilities. These security measures help preserve the system's integrity while shielding sensitive data from unintentional or deliberate exploitation.

By facilitating communication between computers via local and international networks, networking capabilities further increase the usefulness of operating systems. Operating systems control network connections, securely transfer data, enforce communication rules, and arrange for programs to access the internet. The operating system's networking functions are essential for email, web browsing, cloud computing, online gaming, and remote collaboration. Effective network management is becoming a crucial component of operating system design as businesses increasingly depend on distributed computing environments.

Additionally, multitasking is supported by modern operating systems, enabling users to run several programs at once. Users can download files, stream music, access the internet, and send and receive instant messages while editing documents. By effectively handling input handling, memory allocation, processor scheduling, and resource sharing, the operating system manages these tasks. While showcasing the advanced resource management features built into modern operating systems, efficient multitasking increases productivity.

Software engineers can gain important insights by comprehending the connection between operating systems and computer architecture. When performing calculations, efficient programs take into account operating system services, memory utilization, storage access patterns, and processor behavior. Even though they produce accurate data, applications that overuse memory, frequently access storage devices, or disregard processor characteristics may perform poorly. Programmers can therefore improve software by making well-informed design decisions based on how computers actually execute instructions, thanks to their understanding of architecture and operating systems.

Comprehending these fundamental ideas also helps with troubleshooting. Interactions between CPUs, memory, storage devices, operating systems, and applications are frequently involved in performance issues, system crashes, hardware malfunctions, and software disputes. Programmers and system administrators who are aware of these connections are better able to identify issues and implement remedies. They uncover fundamental issues in resource management, hardware constraints, or operating system behavior rather than merely treating symptoms.

Computer architecture and operating systems evolve to accommodate new developments such as cloud computing, virtualization, edge computing, artificial intelligence, and quantum research as computing technology advances. Advanced memory technologies, energy-efficient architectures, multi-core processors, and increasingly complex operating systems all contribute to expanding computational capabilities while preserving compatibility with current software. The basic ideas guiding hardware configuration and operating system administration remain remarkably constant, even as specific technologies evolve.

In the end, understanding computer architecture and operating systems is crucial to comprehending how contemporary computers work on all levels. While operating systems organize these resources to provide effective, safe, and user-friendly computing environments, computer architecture describes how hardware components work together to carry out instructions and process information. Programming, software engineering, cybersecurity, networking, artificial intelligence, and many other computer science fields rely on them as the technological cornerstone. By grasping these ideas, students develop a deeper understanding of computer systems, empowering them to create better software, solve technical problems more effectively, and confidently contribute to the ongoing development of digital technology.

Exploring Databases, Networking, and Internet Technologies

Understanding databases, networking, and internet technologies is crucial to understanding contemporary computer science, as these domains enable computers to store data, communicate with one another, and provide digital services globally. While networking enables devices to share data, databases organize and manage information, programming enables the creation of software applications, and internet technologies link billions of people and systems via a worldwide infrastructure. Together, these technologies enable almost every facet of contemporary life, including social communication, online banking, healthcare, education, entertainment, business, and scientific research. Knowing how these systems work gives students the skills they need to build dependable applications, develop effective digital services, and recognize the intricate technological underpinnings that enable today's connected society.

Databases are structured collections of information that enable computers to store, retrieve, update, and manage data effectively. Since software rarely runs on temporary data alone, every modern program depends on some database. Permanent storage that is accessible long after programs are closed or computers are restarted is necessary for customer records, product inventories, employee information, financial transactions, educational records, medical histories, and social media content. Databases offer organized ways to manage this data while ensuring it is secure, accurate, and accessible throughout its lifecycle.

Before the widespread availability of databases, many apps stored information in simple files. File-based storage remains useful in some situations, but as data volume increases, it becomes more challenging to manage. Redundant data, irregular updates, and constrained search capabilities frequently cause significant difficulties. To solve these issues, databases organize data using carefully designed structures that reduce redundancy and facilitate effective retrieval and modification. Reliability is increased by this methodical arrangement, which also enables multiple users or apps to access the same data simultaneously without causing unnecessary conflicts.

The table is one of the key ideas in database design. A table makes it simpler to store and retrieve structured data by arranging similar information into rows and columns. Usually, a single record is represented by each row, and a particular kind of information about that record is contained in each column. For instance, columns for identification numbers, names, courses, grades, and contact details may be found in a student database. While preserving database integrity, organizing data into tables makes searching, sorting, filtering, and reporting easier. Additionally, as firms gather more data, well-designed tables facilitate future growth.

Databases can organize complex data without needless repetition because of relationships between tables. Related tables share similar IDs that provide meaningful links between records instead of continually storing the same data. An online shopping system might, for example, maintain separate tables for orders, payments, products, and customers, while linking them via distinct identifiers. This method reduces the risk of incorrect data, streamlines updates, and improves storage efficiency. Developers can create databases that remain scalable and orderly even as applications become more complex by developing a thorough understanding of relationships.

The tools needed to develop, maintain, secure, and administer databases are provided by database management systems (DBMS). These systems let developers concentrate on application logic rather than low-level storage issues by managing storage organization, user access, transaction processing, backup mechanisms, and data recovery. Multiple users can work with shared data simultaneously while maintaining accuracy and consistency thanks to a database management system. Additionally, it offers methods to limit access so that only those with proper authorization can view or modify private data.

The standard language for interacting with relational databases is called Structured Query Language, or SQL. Through carefully crafted commands, SQL enables users and applications to access information, add new records, edit existing data, and remove out-of-date entries. Developers use SQL statements to retrieve precisely the information they require rather than manually searching through thousands or millions of data points. With effective access to stored data, these queries enable firms to create reports, analyze consumer behavior, monitor inventory, and support decision-making. SQL's basic principles are relatively constant across the industry, despite minor variations in syntax among database platforms.

One of the most crucial duties of database systems is data integrity. For financial transactions, medical diagnosis, educational records, inventory management, and a host of other crucial functions, organizations rely on correct information. As a result, databases apply rules that ensure related records remain consistent and prevent erroneous information from being saved. Reliable data is maintained even when multiple users access the system simultaneously, thanks to validation processes, limitations, and transaction management. These measures encourage trust in stored data while shielding companies from expensive mistakes.

Because databases can contain sensitive personal, financial, medical, and organizational data, security is equally crucial. Database systems use user rights, encryption methods, authentication procedures, and auditing tools to prevent unwanted access to or alteration of sensitive data. In accordance with company standards, administrators carefully specify which people are permitted to see, edit, or remove particular data. Effective database security has become a crucial part of responsible information management as cyber dangers continue to rise.

The communication infrastructure that allows computers to share data is provided by networking. Because they can share resources, collaborate on projects, access remote services, and communicate quickly over long distances, individual computers become much more powerful when connected to a network. Networks can be as tiny as a few devices in a residential setting or as large as global infrastructures that support billions of computers. Gaining an understanding of networking principles enables students to understand how information moves effectively between systems and supports the daily use of digital services.

A computer network is made up of linked devices that use standard communication techniques to exchange data. Computers, cellphones, servers, printers, routers, switches, and a variety of specialized systems are examples of these devices. Depending on the network design, communication can take place via satellite transmissions, fiber-optic links, wireless communications, or physical wires. Networking depends on well-defined protocols that set common guidelines for dependable information exchange between various hardware and software platforms, regardless of the transmission medium.

Communication protocols provide the standardized language that enables various devices to communicate with one another. Computers from different manufacturers would find it difficult to share information efficiently without common protocols. During communication, protocols specify how data should be prepared, sent, received, validated, and acknowledged. These standards facilitate reliable information sharing between local networks and the global Internet while ensuring interoperability across billions of connected devices. The unseen basis of contemporary digital communication consists of well-established protocols.

Devices in comparatively small geographic regions, such as homes, offices, schools, or university campuses, are connected by local area networks. Users can effectively share data, printers, internet connections, and computer resources thanks to these networks. Local networks typically offer fast communication speeds and dependable performance because devices stay physically close to one another. To facilitate employee collaboration while centralizing access to shared apps and organizational databases, businesses primarily rely on local networks.

By joining several small networks, wide-area networks enable communication over much wider geographic areas. Wide-area networks are frequently used by government agencies, educational institutions, multinational enterprises, and national organizations to coordinate operations across geographically dispersed locations. To ensure dependable communication over great distances, these networks usually make use of satellite connections, fiber-optic infrastructure, leased communication lines, or internet-based technology. Despite their physical isolation, businesses can function as a single cohesive entity thanks to wide-area networking.

The biggest and most significant computer network ever established is the Internet. The Internet is made up of numerous interconnected networks run by governments, corporations, academic organizations, and service providers worldwide rather than operating as a single, centralized system. This distributed design supports massive amounts of communication while enhancing reliability by enabling information to flow across multiple channels. The Internet is one of humanity's greatest technological achievements since billions of people rely on it for social contact, education, business, entertainment, healthcare, and research.

Among the internet technologies that users are most familiar with are websites and web applications. A website is made up of linked digital pages that can be accessed via web browsers to provide services, information, or interactive experiences. These features are expanded by contemporary web programs that facilitate online banking, commerce, education, teamwork, and entertainment. Programming, databases, networking, and server technologies all work together to send information to users worldwide in a timely and dependable manner.

Because they store website material and handle user requests, web servers are essential to internet communication. When a user inputs a website address into a browser, the request is sent over the Internet to the relevant server. After retrieving the requested data and completing any required database operations, the server sends the results back to the user's device. Despite requiring communication over thousands of kilometers and multiple intermediary network nodes, the complete operation frequently takes place in fractions of a second.

By enabling apps, storage, and processing resources to operate remotely rather than relying solely on local hardware, cloud computing has drastically changed internet technologies. Users are increasingly using web browsers or mobile devices to access apps rather than installing software on their personal PCs, with processing activities handled by distant data centers. With the flexibility, scalability, automatic upgrades, and efficient resource use that cloud services offer, businesses can respond quickly to changing needs without maintaining a large physical infrastructure.

By enabling automatic communication between various software systems, Application Programming Interfaces, or APIs, significantly increase the possibilities of the Internet. Applications can request services, exchange data, and incorporate features without direct human intervention thanks to APIs. APIs can be used, for instance, by an online shopping application to display interactive maps, retrieve weather forecasts, calculate shipping costs, and process electronic payments. Through reusable services, these standardized interfaces promote software compatibility and speed up development.

Because connected systems are constantly at risk of fraud, malware, unauthorized access, and data theft, cybersecurity remains a crucial factor across databases, networking, and internet technologies. Digital data is protected during storage and transmission via firewalls, encryption, authentication, intrusion detection systems, and secure communication protocols. To create systems that protect individual privacy, corporate assets, and public confidence while preserving dependable access for authorized users, responsible technology professionals must comprehend security principles.

In networked applications, performance improvement is also crucial. Developers must create databases, networks, and internet services that can function effectively under demanding workloads as user populations and information volumes rise. Database indexing, load balancing, caching, content delivery networks, and efficient communication protocols are a few strategies that increase responsiveness while reducing user wait times. As demand grows, careful planning ensures that applications remain dependable and scalable.

The integration of databases, networking, and internet technologies has enabled numerous opportunities for innovation across almost every business. Healthcare institutions facilitate remote consultations while managing electronic medical records. Throughout the world, educational institutions provide students with online learning opportunities. Companies run international e-commerce platforms that simultaneously serve millions of consumers. While researchers collaborate globally through shared scientific databases and high-speed communication networks, governments provide digital public services. To gather, process, and disseminate vast amounts of data, emerging technologies such as artificial intelligence, the Internet of Things, and smart cities further rely on these fundamental processes.

In the end, investigating databases, networking, and internet technologies provides crucial insight into the infrastructure that sustains the modern digital world. Networking facilitates connections between devices, databases organize and safeguard important data, and internet technologies provide robust digital services that link people and systems worldwide. These technologies work together to form the foundation of contemporary computing, enabling software programs to securely transmit data, store information effectively, and deliver meaningful experiences to billions of users. By comprehending these interrelated ideas, students gain the skills necessary to create scalable apps, handle data ethically, and confidently contribute to the ongoing development of technology in a world that is becoming more interconnected by the day.

Understanding Software Engineering Principles and Development Practices

The methodical process of creating, testing, deploying, and maintaining software systems that are dependable, effective, safe, and capable of satisfying user needs is known as software engineering. Software engineering encompasses the broader processes, principles, and approaches needed to produce high-quality software throughout its entire lifecycle, whereas programming is primarily concerned with writing code. Millions of lines of code, several development teams, intricate integrations, and frequent upgrades are common components of modern apps. It takes much more than just technical programming skills to handle this complexity successfully. It necessitates meticulous planning, well-structured workflows, efficient communication, quality control, and long-term thinking. Programmers can go beyond merely writing functional programs and start developing software that is scalable, maintainable, and beneficial for many years by grasping software engineering ideas and development techniques.

Software engineering's focus on methodically resolving real-world issues is one of its distinguishing features. Identifying a need, comprehending the users of the program, and figuring out how technology might offer a workable answer are the first steps in any software project. Software engineers spend a lot of time gathering requirements, analyzing objectives, identifying limitations, and understanding customer expectations rather than writing code immediately. This planning phase helps prevent misunderstandings and guarantees that the finished solution solves the right issue rather than adding extraneous features. Effective software engineering starts long before the first line of code is written, as careful analysis reduces costly redesign efforts later in the development process.

Every successful software project starts with requirements analysis since it determines what the program must do. While nonfunctional requirements include attributes such as performance, security, dependability, usability, and scalability, functional requirements specify the capabilities and services the program must provide. Both categories are equally crucial since customers may not be satisfied with software that has the right functions but operates slowly or has insufficient security. To reconcile competing priorities, set clear expectations, and produce comprehensive specifications that guide future development efforts, software engineers collaborate extensively with stakeholders. Clear specifications lower ambiguity and offer quantifiable standards by which finished software can be assessed.

Software engineers gather requirements and then proceed to the design phase, where they decide on the internal organization of the system. System architecture component interactions, data management, and user interfaces are all defined by software design, which turns abstract concepts into organized blueprints. Good design anticipates future expansion and changing needs while emphasizing simplicity, flexibility, and maintainability. Instead of writing a single, massive block of code, engineers brake systems into smaller modules, each responsible for a specific task. This modular structure facilitates cooperation, makes testing easier, enhances readability, and permits component updates without affecting the program as a whole.

One of the core design tenets of software engineering is the separation of concerns. Instead of merging unrelated tasks into a single module, this idea encourages developers to give each component a clearly defined responsibility. For instance, database modules should handle data storage, business logic should handle application rules and decision-making, and user interface components should concentrate on information presentation. By keeping these tasks apart, complexity is decreased, maintainability is enhanced, and future changes are made much simpler. Developers can find issues faster and launch new features with more assurance when each component completes a single, clearly defined mission.

Because it enables developers to control complexity by concentrating on key ideas while concealing superfluous implementation details, abstraction is also crucial to software engineering. Software systems are frequently made up of many interdependent parts, each with complex internal logic. Programmers can use these components through clearly defined interfaces without needing to understand every internal function, thanks to abstraction. For instance, developers don't need to learn every algorithm to use database libraries, networking frameworks, or encryption tools. This method speeds up development, promotes code reuse, and frees teams to focus on more complex issues rather than continually implementing common functionality.

By safeguarding the internal state and behavior of software components, encapsulation enhances abstraction. Through carefully crafted interfaces, encapsulation limits interaction rather than permitting free access to every variable and function. This restricted access lessens interdependence between various program components and eliminates unintentional changes to important data. Developers can therefore alter or enhance internal implementations without affecting other components that depend solely on the published interface. Thus, encapsulation greatly enhances program stability, maintainability, and long-term flexibility.

Modularity, which divides software into different components that can be created, tested, and maintained independently, is another fundamental idea. Because each module concentrates on a certain set of tasks, modular systems are simpler to comprehend. Additionally, they facilitate collaboration, enabling several teams of developers to operate concurrently without interfering with one another. Because it prevents applications from becoming unmanageable collections of closely related code, modularity becomes more crucial as software grows. Clearly specified interfaces enable well-designed modules to communicate while reducing superfluous dependencies that complicate maintenance.

Another important goal of software engineering is reusability. Instead of fixing the same problems over and over again, developers design components that can be used in different parts of the same program or across multiple projects. By offering tried-and-true answers to typical programming problems, functions, libraries, frameworks, and application programming interfaces all encourage reuse. Reusable components promote uniformity across software systems, shorten development times, and increase reliability through repeated testing. Instead of replicating previous work, this idea enables engineers to concentrate their creativity on addressing novel issues.

From initial planning to long-term maintenance, the software development lifecycle offers an organized framework for project management. Most development lifecycles include phases such as planning, requirements analysis, design, implementation, testing, deployment, and maintenance, though individual approaches differ. Each stage ensures that development remains structured and quantifiable while enhancing the overall quality of the project. Teams can better coordinate tasks, allocate resources, and identify potential hazards before they become serious issues by adhering to a planned lifecycle. Additionally, it offers opportunities to assess progress and refine project goals.

Depending on the company's goals and the project's features, different software development techniques offer different approaches to project management. Conventional sequential approaches provide comprehensive documentation and predictable planning, emphasizing finishing each development step before starting the next. Iterative and incremental approaches, on the other hand, split projects into smaller development cycles and produce functional software more frequently. Agile approaches promote ongoing cooperation, frequent feedback, and adaptability to shifting needs. Agile teams adjust their priorities in response to user input and changing business requirements, rather than treating plans as set in stone. Software engineers can choose methods that best fit particular project contexts by having a thorough understanding of various development approaches.

Since a single developer is rarely involved in modern software projects, teamwork is essential to software engineering. To create high-quality software, successful teams depend on efficient communication, shared responsibility, and well-coordinated planning. Throughout the project lifecycle, specialized knowledge is contributed by developers, designers, testers, project managers, business analysts, and stakeholders. Everyone stays aligned with the project's goals through frequent discussions, documentation, design reviews, and collaborative problem-solving. Additionally, effective communication minimizes misconceptions that could otherwise lead to costly mistakes or delays.

Because version control systems log changes made to source code over time, they are essential to collaborative software development. Developers may examine older iterations, compare changes, restore earlier implementations, and coordinate contributions from other team members thanks to these systems, which save historical records of every alteration. Version control makes it easier to collaborate on big projects and significantly lowers the chance of losing important work. Additionally, it encourages experimentation since developers can safely test new concepts without permanently altering the core software coding until enhancements are confirmed.

Throughout software engineering, code quality is always a top concern. If the final software is hard to comprehend, alter, or maintain, writing functional code alone is insufficient. Clarity, consistency, efficiency, and simplicity are key components of high-quality code. Readability is enhanced by logical organization, informative documentation, uniform formatting, well-organized functions, and meaningful variable names. Software engineers understand that people who did not write the code will frequently maintain it for many years. As a result, having a clear organization becomes an investment in software dependability and future productivity.

Because it confirms that software meets both functional and nonfunctional criteria, testing is another essential component of software engineering. Normal functioning, boundary conditions, unexpected inputs, performance characteristics, security flaws, and system dependability are all examined in effective testing. Several testing methods assess software from various angles, including individual components, integrated systems, and the full user experience. Because it enables repeated verification anytime code changes, automated testing has been especially helpful in ensuring that new features do not inadvertently harm old functionality. Thorough testing boosts user confidence in the finished product and dramatically lowers problems.

Because programs must adapt to evolving technology, user expectations, and organizational requirements, software maintenance continues long after initial deployment. Correcting found flaws, boosting performance, strengthening security, adjusting to new hardware or operating systems, and adding new functionality are all examples of maintenance tasks. Maintainability is one of the most crucial factors considered during initial design, since many software systems remain in active use for decades. Because its well-organized structure reduces the impact of changes across unrelated components, well-engineered software can more easily accommodate future alterations.

Instead of being an optional factor added after development, security is now a crucial component of software engineering. Sensitive financial, medical, educational, and personal data are often managed by modern applications that need to be protected against unauthorized access. Throughout the development process, safe software engineering integrates authentication, authorization, encryption, input validation, secure communication, and vulnerability assessment. By addressing security early on, risks are decreased, and consumers, businesses, and vital infrastructure are shielded from increasingly complex cyberattacks.

Decisions made in software engineering are also influenced by performance optimization. While delivering responsive user experiences, efficient software makes responsible use of processor power, memory, storage, and network resources. To find areas for improvement, engineers examine data structures, algorithms, communication styles, and resource usage. Optimization should, however, be carefully balanced against readability and maintainability, as overly complex optimizations may add needless complexity without significant practical advantages. Effective engineering seeks solutions that maintain comprehensibility and flexibility while delivering adequate performance.

Every step of the software engineering process is supported by documentation, which tracks requirements, design choices, implementation details, testing protocols, and maintenance tasks. New team members may easily grasp current systems thanks to well-prepared documentation, which also serves as a useful resource for future improvements. By ensuring shared knowledge of project objectives and implementation techniques, technical documentation also helps developers, testers, managers, and stakeholders communicate. Even though it takes more work, documentation greatly increases a project's sustainability over the long run.

Since software today affects almost every facet of society, professional ethics are becoming increasingly relevant in software engineering. When creating digital systems, engineers must take social responsibility, privacy, security, accessibility, fairness, and dependability into account. Millions of users could be affected by decisions made during development; therefore, moral judgment is just as crucial as technical proficiency. Responsible software engineering places a high priority on user welfare, safeguards private data, complies with legal requirements, and aims to reduce unintentional harm caused by technological systems.

Another quality that distinguishes excellent software engineers is their constant learning. Cloud platforms, programming languages, frameworks, development tools, security procedures, and industry standards are all continuously changing. As a result, professionals develop lifelong learning habits by researching new technologies, trying out novel approaches, engaging with technical groups, and reflecting on completed projects. This dedication to continuous development guarantees that developers maintain their flexibility while producing efficient software in quickly evolving technical settings.

In the end, developing software that is not just functional but also dependable, maintainable, secure, and scalable requires an understanding of software engineering principles and development techniques. With careful planning, well-organized design, productive teamwork, rigorous testing, and ongoing improvement, programming is transformed from the solitary act of writing code into a disciplined engineering process. Aspiring developers acquire the skills and habits required to create expert software systems that continue to provide value throughout their entire lifecycle by embracing principles such as modularity, abstraction, encapsulation, reusability, quality assurance, security, documentation, and ethical responsibility. These engineering techniques remain crucial for developing cutting-edge solutions that customers can rely on, businesses can sustain, and upcoming developers can safely expand as technology evolves. Software becomes increasingly integrated into contemporary culture.

CHAPTER IV
Applying Computer Science Through Practical Projects

Designing Real-World Software Applications

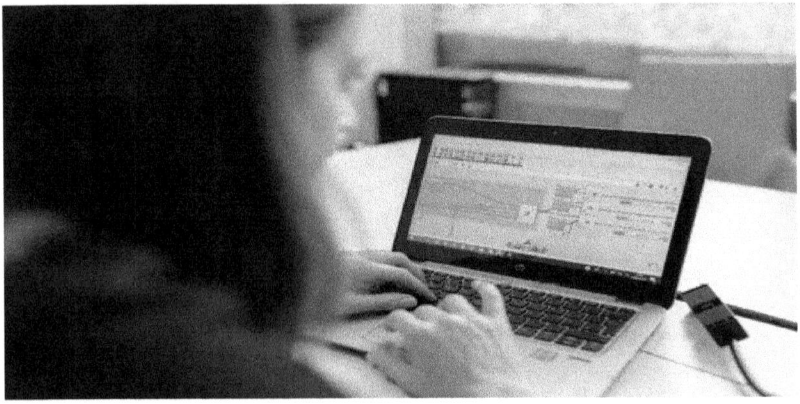

The process of turning concepts, user requirements, and corporate objectives into workable digital solutions that address significant issues is known as real-world software application design. The technical basis for software development is provided by studying programming languages and methods, but creating complete applications requires far more comprehensive thinking. Developers need to understand how people use technology, efficiently organize data, design reliable system architectures, ensure security, and plan for future expansion. Successful software programs are evaluated based on how well they assist users in achieving their objectives while remaining stable, maintainable, and user-friendly, rather than on how many features they have. Aspiring computer scientists can develop software that offers enduring value in both personal and professional contexts by grasping the fundamentals of application design.

Finding a real problem that technology can answer is the first step in any successful software development. Instead of developing software just because it is technically feasible, developers first assess user needs and determine how an application can increase productivity, streamline complex tasks, or offer new features. Information is gathered during this stage through observation, interviews, studies, and conversations with potential consumers. Developers ensure their software meets real-world demands rather than adding needless complexity by being aware of the difficulties consumers encounter. A project's development time is often shortened, and the quality of the end application is enhanced by careful planning at the outset.

One of the most crucial phases in the design of software applications is requirements analysis. Developers specify the goals of the application, its features, and the performance, dependability, and security standards that users anticipate. While nonfunctional requirements address attributes such as speed, scalability, usability, and maintainability, functional requirements specify the precise tasks the software must perform. Well-documented requirements guide the development process and help prevent misunderstandings that can lead to expensive changes later on.

The target audience greatly influences design choices. The technical expertise, expectations, and working circumstances of various user groups vary. A distinct interface is needed for an application meant for youngsters than for financial analysts or medical specialists. When creating interfaces and workflows, developers take accessibility, language, experience, and typical user duties into account. By maintaining software's intuitiveness, user-centered design reduces frustration and boosts productivity and satisfaction.

Before implementation starts, developers can arrange software into manageable components by planning the application's architecture. Applications are separated into several modules, each responsible for a particular task, rather than producing a single, massive collection of linked code. Databases store information, communication modules exchange data with external services, business logic interprets application rules, and user interface components oversee user interaction. This modular structure makes software easier to understand while streamlining development, testing, maintenance, and future growth.

Because most software relies on dependable information management, database architecture is another crucial component of practical applications. Customer accounts, inventory records, financial transactions, educational information, appointments, and communication history are frequently stored in applications. Developers meticulously arrange this data into logical structures that facilitate effective storage and retrieval while reducing needless duplication. As information develops over time, well-designed databases facilitate future improvements, preserve data consistency, and optimize application performance.

Every software application's visible component, the user interface, has a significant impact on user satisfaction. Clear information is presented, controls are arranged rationally, and users are guided naturally through various activities by effective interfaces. For users to rapidly grasp how to use the application, buttons, menus, forms, and navigation methods should all act consistently. Clear feedback, accessible writing, relevant labels, and straightforward design all contribute to less misunderstanding and more fruitful interaction. Effective interface design keeps software both aesthetically pleasing and useful by striking a balance between practical usage and visual appeal.

By taking into account how users feel when engaging with software, user experience goes beyond looks. Applications should respond quickly, provide helpful messages, avoid common problems, and gracefully recover from them. While error messages should include clear explanations of issues rather than technical jargon that is difficult for users to grasp, lengthy operations should show progress indications. Developers create programs that users love and trust for critical tasks by anticipating their needs and minimizing frustration.

Because modern applications often handle sensitive personal, financial, and organizational data, security has emerged as one of the most significant duties in software design. Developers put in place permission rules that restrict access to resources that are protected, authentication systems that confirm user identities, and encryption techniques that safeguard private information while it is being transmitted and stored. By ensuring that all supplied data adheres to specified formats, input validation prevents deliberate or unintentional misuse. Reducing vulnerabilities that could jeopardize software stability and protecting users are two benefits of integrating security throughout the design process.

Another crucial factor to take into account while designing an application is performance. No matter how much data is stored or how many users are accessing the system at once, users want software to respond quickly. To increase responsiveness, developers optimize database operations, algorithms, memory use, and communication procedures. Optimization shouldn't, however, make the program unduly complex. The greatest designs strike a balance among readability, speed, and maintainability, making it easier for future developers to understand and improve the program.

Applications are guaranteed to continue operating efficiently as demand rises thanks to scalability. A successful program might serve thousands or even millions of users after starting with a modest user base. By creating systems that can manage bigger databases, more users, more network traffic, and more functionality without necessitating a total redesign, developers prepare for this expansion. Early scalability planning enables software to develop organically while preserving dependable performance as businesses expand.

When creating dependable software, testing is a crucial component. Developers test every feature to ensure it functions properly in both typical and uncommon scenarios. To identify flaws before deployment, testing examines user interactions, performance, security, compatibility, and error handling. Software quality is maintained throughout continuous development through automated testing, which enables repeated verification whenever changes are made. Thorough testing reduces maintenance costs while increasing confidence that the program will function reliably in real-world settings.

Every step of the software development process is supported by documentation, which tracks details on database structures, programming interfaces, system architecture, configuration methods, and maintenance needs. Technical documentation helps future developers responsible for developing or maintaining the software, while user documentation describes how to use the application efficiently. Confusion is decreased, new team member onboarding is made easier, and long-term project sustainability is enhanced by well-organized documentation.

When creating practical applications, teamwork is equally crucial. Teams comprising developers, designers, testers, project managers, and business stakeholders work on the majority of professional software projects. Everyone will have a common knowledge of the project's objectives, technical choices, and development priorities if there is effective communication. Frequent conversations, code reviews, and project planning meetings promote knowledge sharing among team members and enhance software quality.

Because applications must adjust to evolving technology, user expectations, and business requirements, maintenance is necessary even after software has been published. Based on customer feedback, developers enhance performance, increase security, fix found flaws, and add new features. Modular architecture, well-structured code, and unambiguous documentation make it considerably easier for applications to adapt to these changes than disorganized systems. Thus, one of the most beneficial investments made during early development is designing for maintainability.

Another crucial component of software application design is ethical responsibility. Education, healthcare, communication, banking, transportation, and many other facets of society are impacted by modern software. Throughout the design process, developers must take privacy, equity, accessibility, openness, and responsible data management into account. Applications should safeguard user data, refrain from discriminatory actions, and continue to be usable by people of various backgrounds and abilities. In addition to ensuring that technology progress serves society ethically, ethical software design increases public trust.

Writing functional code alone is not enough to develop real-world software applications. Technical proficiency is combined with careful planning, user-centered thinking, well-organized architecture, efficient communication, security, testing, documentation, and ongoing improvement. Every successful application is the result of thoughtful choices made to address significant real-world issues while balancing usability, performance, stability, scalability, and maintainability. Aspiring computer scientists can acquire the knowledge and practical skills necessary to produce software that efficiently serves people, businesses, and communities by grasping these ideas. The ability to create dependable, safe, and user-focused applications remains one of the most important and enduring skills in computer science as technology advances and digital systems become increasingly integrated into daily life.

Working with APIs, Libraries, and Development Tools

Since producing software rarely entails coding every component from scratch, working with APIs, libraries, and development tools is a crucial skill for modern software engineers. Rather, programmers expand upon pre-existing technologies that offer dependable, tested, and reusable functionality. With these resources, developers can focus on resolving specific issues while leveraging the expertise of other engineers who have spent years developing tools, frameworks, and services. Programmers frequently work with application programming interfaces, software libraries, and specialized development tools that speed up development, enhance quality, and make complex tasks easier, whether they are creating desktop software, mobile applications, websites, cloud services, or embedded systems. Developers can efficiently design complex programs while preserving flexibility, dependability, and long-term maintainability by comprehending how these resources operate.

An established collection of guidelines and procedures that enables communication between various software systems is known as an application programming interface, or API for short. An API offers thoughtfully constructed access points through which other programs can request information or perform specific tasks, rather than exposing every internal detail of an application. Software developed by many organizations, written in various programming languages, or operating on various platforms, can coexist harmoniously through managed communication. Because APIs facilitate integration, automation, and interoperability across a wide range of digital systems, they have emerged as one of the most crucial pillars of contemporary software development.

Considering an API as a waiter in a restaurant is one way to comprehend it. Clients do not go into the kitchen to make their own meals. Rather, customers make orders via the waiter, who then notifies the kitchen and returns the finished dish. Similarly, software programs send requests to an API, which interacts with the underlying system and either completes the intended task or returns the requested data. Because users of the API do not need to comprehend the internal workings of the service they are accessing, this separation streamlines interactions. They merely adhere to the interface's established guidelines.

APIs are essential to many daily tasks in modern applications. Using APIs, a weather application obtains forecasts from internet weather sources. To finish financial transactions, an online shopping platform interacts with payment processors. Mapping services provide navigational and geographic data to mapping applications. Through standardized interfaces, social media platforms enable users to exchange content across many services. For authentication, cloud storage, messaging, notifications, analytics, and a host of other features, even basic mobile applications often rely on APIs. These integrations show how developers can integrate specialized services into all-encompassing digital solutions using APIs.

By dividing functionality into separate services, APIs encourage modular program design. Developers can divide up the work across specialized systems linked by clear interfaces rather than integrating every feature into a single application. Because individual services can be upgraded, altered, or expanded without necessitating significant modifications to the applications that rely on them, this strategy increases flexibility. By enabling various services to run on distinct hardware resources based on demand, it also promotes scalability. APIs continue to be crucial in facilitating effective communication between linked software components as businesses embrace distributed computing systems.

One of the most crucial elements of using APIs is documentation. Developers rely on precise documentation outlining available operations, necessary inputs, expected outputs, authentication processes, error responses, and usage restrictions because they work with systems they did not design. By offering precise instructions for integrating external services, well-written documentation drastically reduces development time. Therefore, mastering the ability to read and comprehend technical documentation is a crucial professional skill that applies to almost every facet of software engineering, not just APIs. Programmers can confidently use advanced technologies without having to understand their entire internal implementations thanks to effective documentation.

Because many interfaces give users access to sensitive data or useful services, security is especially crucial when using APIs. While authorization systems determine which actions specific programs are allowed to perform, authentication techniques verify the identity of applications requesting access. Usage restrictions prevent excessive requests that could overload systems, and secure communication protocols protect transmitted data from unauthorized interception. By safeguarding authentication credentials, verifying received data, and adhering to service provider-defined access limitations, responsible developers adhere to established security protocols.

Another crucial tool for contemporary programming is software libraries. A library is an assemblage of prewritten code that addresses typical programming problems. Developers use libraries with tested functionality for tasks like mathematical calculations, graphical user interfaces, networking, file management, encryption, image processing, and database communication instead of building each algorithm or utility separately. By enabling programmers to build on existing knowledge rather than continually tackling the same problems, libraries save time, increase reliability, and reduce development costs.

One of the biggest benefits that software libraries provide is reusability. It is inefficient for each programmer to create their own implementation because many computing tasks are duplicated in several applications. Libraries that process photos, compress files, modify dates, or do statistical analysis, for instance, can support hundreds of different applications with little modification. These libraries frequently offer superior quality and greater reliability than newly written alternatives, as they undergo rigorous testing and ongoing refinement. Therefore, reusing tried-and-true components greatly increases software stability while freeing engineers to focus on application-specific needs.

Additionally, libraries encourage uniformity among software projects. Standardized libraries are frequently created by organizations to handle common tasks like configuration management, communication, security, and logging. By eliminating redundant work and simplifying maintenance, shared libraries guarantee that programs adhere to standard procedures. Modifying a centralized library helps all applications that rely on it when security updates or upgrades are needed, rather than requiring individual changes across several projects. Large development teams may handle software more effectively thanks to this centralized method.

Rather than picking the first library that comes up, choosing the right one involves considerable consideration. Before integrating external components into their systems, developers consider factors such as reliability, documentation quality, community support, performance, compatibility, licensing terms, security history, and long-term maintenance. Because they receive frequent updates, bug fixes, and security enhancements, well-known libraries maintained by vibrant development communities often inspire greater confidence. Therefore, responsible software engineering entails striking a balance between ease of use and a thorough evaluation of potential hazards and future maintenance needs.

Development tools provide the software environment that facilitates each step of the application creation process. Development tools assist programmers in writing, organizing, testing, debugging, analyzing, and deploying software more effectively, while programming languages specify how code is written. Over the years, these technologies have undergone significant change, shifting software development from simple hand-edited text files to complex engineering processes supported by automation, visualization, teamwork, and intelligent support. Programmers can boost efficiency while upholding high standards of software quality by being aware of development tools.

IDEs, or integrated development environments, integrate many programming tools into a single workspace. Developers may modify code, compile programs, troubleshoot issues, and manage projects all inside a single integrated environment instead of moving between several applications. Software development is made much easier by modern IDEs' syntax highlighting, automatic code completion, project structure, error detection, debugging help, and navigation functions. These features free up programmers to concentrate more on problem-solving and application design by reducing repetitive activities.

Additionally, code editors are useful development tools, especially for projects that require support for multiple programming languages or for lightweight environments. Modern code editors offer strong capabilities such as intelligent text editing, plugin support, grammar checking, version control integration, and customized workflows, even though they are typically less complete than full integrated development environments. Effective software development relies more on disciplined methods than on any specific tool, as evidenced by the fact that many developers choose editing environments based on corporate rules, project requirements, or personal preferences.

Programmers can find and fix software flaws methodically using debugging tools. Developers use interactive debuggers to watch program execution step by step, examine variable values, track memory usage, and assess logical conditions at runtime rather than relying solely on printed output or guesswork. These features improve comprehension of program behavior while significantly simplifying the analysis of complicated issues. By allowing developers to precisely detect problems rather than making needless changes through trial and error, the efficient use of debugging tools greatly improves software quality.

By automating verification processes that would otherwise require significant manual labor, testing tools further increase program reliability. Every time software is modified, automated testing frameworks repeatedly run prewritten test cases to ensure that current functionality continues to work properly and to identify newly introduced flaws. While security analysis tools find potential flaws that need to be fixed before release, performance testing tools assess an application's responsiveness under high workloads. Organizations can lower long-term maintenance costs and enhance software quality by incorporating automated testing into routine development efforts.

Another essential class of development tools is version control systems. These systems preserve comprehensive histories of source code updates, enabling developers to examine past iterations, compare changes, restore earlier implementations, and collaborate efficiently. Because version control allows programmers to securely test new concepts without permanently altering reliable software, it encourages innovation. Synchronizing contributions from several developers working concurrently on common projects, it also makes teamwork easier. Version control is an essential part of contemporary development workflows in almost all professional software organizations.

Build tools automate the process of turning source code into executable programs. Compiling many files, resolving library dependencies, packaging resources, running tests, and creating deployment artifacts are all common tasks for large software projects. It would take a lot of time and be error-prone to complete these activities by hand. By carrying out defined processes each time software is ready for testing or release, build automation guarantees consistency. Automation improves reliability in a variety of development contexts while reducing repetitive effort.

The process of acquiring, maintaining, and arranging external libraries needed for software projects is made easier by dependency management technologies. Hundreds of reusable components maintained by several organizations are often necessary for modern applications. Dependency management solutions track relationships between libraries, automatically fetch compatible versions, and streamline updates when new features become available. These tools help developers maintain safe, up-to-date software environments while reducing setup complexity.

As software development teams spread across several geographical sites, collaboration technologies have grown in significance. Programmers, testers, designers, managers, and stakeholders can coordinate their efforts with the use of communication platforms, issue tracking systems, project management software, and documentation repositories. Organizational efficiency increases, and misunderstandings decrease when there is shared visibility into project progress, development priorities, identified flaws, and planned enhancements. Throughout the software development lifecycle, efficient collaboration technologies promote accountability, transparency, and coordinated decision-making.

The significance of development automation is further illustrated by continuous integration and continuous deployment techniques. Continuous integration automatically runs tests to verify software reliability while routinely merging contributions from multiple developers into a shared codebase. By preparing validated software for release with little manual involvement, continuous deployment expands this automation. These procedures reduce integration issues, accelerate feedback, improve software quality, and enable businesses to release upgrades quickly while preserving program reliability.

Because technology is constantly evolving, mastering APIs, libraries, and programming tools also promotes lifelong learning. Regularly, new frameworks, programming languages, cloud services, automation platforms, and development environments are created to meet evolving market demands and offer enhanced capabilities. By reviewing documentation, experimenting with new technologies, engaging in technical forums, and consistently honing their professional skills, successful developers foster curiosity and adaptability. Regardless of changes in technology, this openness to learning guarantees long-term efficacy.

In the end, a key component of contemporary software engineering is working with APIs, libraries, and development tools. Libraries offer reusable solutions to common programming problems, APIs facilitate communication across separate software systems, and development tools expedite all phases of application development, testing, deployment, and maintenance. When used, these tools help developers create complex software more quickly while enhancing scalability, dependability, and maintainability. Programmers gain critical skills that enable them to create real-world applications that can satisfy the demands of today's interconnected digital landscape by learning how to integrate external services, assess reusable components, and make effective use of professional development environments. These technologies show that successful software development involves integrating knowledge, teamwork, and reusable innovation to provide solutions that are effective, reliable, and beneficial to consumers worldwide.

Building Web, Desktop, and Automation Projects

One of the best ways to turn theoretical computer science knowledge into practical skills is to build online, desktop, and automation projects. A solid academic foundation is provided by learning programming ideas, algorithms, data structures, and software engineering principles; however, genuine knowledge emerges when these concepts are applied to practical issues. Projects push students to think critically, integrate multiple technologies, and address real-world challenges that aren't always possible to tackle with brief programming exercises. Whether constructing an automated tool, a desktop program, or an interactive website, every project enhances problem-solving skills, fosters creativity, and boosts confidence in software development.

Because web-based software can be accessed through web browsers across a variety of devices and operating systems, web application development has emerged as one of the most popular fields in contemporary programming. Web apps are vital to everyday life, ranging from financial services and healthcare portals to online retailers and educational platforms. Developing web applications introduces key concepts such as client-server communication, database integration, user authentication, and responsive interface design, while helping students understand how people interact with software over the internet. These projects show how many technologies cooperate to provide users worldwide with dependable digital experiences.

Understanding the target users' needs is one of the first things to consider when developing a website. Successful web apps are built with efficient problem-solving in mind rather than just technical characteristics. Developers start by determining the needs of users, organizing the functionality of the program, and creating user-friendly interfaces that naturally lead users through various tasks. Regardless of technical expertise, customers expect websites and online apps to be user-friendly; thus, simplicity, consistency, and accessibility become crucial considerations. While increasing overall user pleasure, careful planning during the design process helps minimize future development issues.

Since most contemporary apps rely on structured data storage, database integration is another crucial component of many online projects. Reliable databases that can effectively store and retrieve data are necessary for customer accounts, product inventories, educational records, reservations, and communication history. Developers get knowledge on how to logically arrange data, implement secure user information management techniques, and establish linkages between various records. By understanding database integration, students can create applications that are scalable, well-organized, and capable of handling increasing volumes of data over time.

During web development, security is also a major concern. Developers must safeguard users against illegal access and data breaches because many applications handle financial or personal data. Encryption protects sensitive data in transit, authorization controls determine access permissions, and authentication systems verify user identities. By ensuring that submitted data adheres to expected formats, input validation helps prevent harmful attacks. Early exposure to these security concepts promotes responsible software development and fosters user and application confidence.

Despite the rapid development of web technology, desktop apps still play a significant role. Desktop programs operate directly on a computer's operating system, in contrast to browser-based software, and often provide greater access to local hardware resources, data, and computing power. Desktop software is used in many areas, including scientific and analytical tools, engineering applications, accounting systems, office productivity software, and multimedia editing programs. By developing desktop projects, students can gain a clear understanding of how software interacts with operating systems and creates apps that can run without constant internet access.

One of the most satisfying parts of developing desktop applications is creating efficient graphical user interfaces. To help users do tasks effectively, developers design windows, menus, forms, buttons, dialog boxes, and navigation systems. Every design choice affects usability, from where controls are located to how instructions and error messages are written. Positive user experiences, less confusion, and shorter learning times are all produced by well-designed interfaces. By creating desktop programs, students gain valuable experience in striking a balance among usefulness, visual simplicity, and usability.

Another crucial component that is often included in desktop programs is file management. Documents and other digital data stored on local devices can be created, edited, organized, saved, and retrieved using a variety of apps. Developers learn how to handle various file types, organize directories, read and write files, and safeguard important user data from unintentional loss. While highlighting the significance of information protection throughout the program lifecycle, backup features, automatic saving methods, and error recovery procedures enhance application reliability.

By allowing computers to perform repetitive tasks automatically, automation initiatives present another useful area of software development. Organizing files, processing documents, creating reports, monitoring systems, and transferring data between programs are just a few of the daily tasks that require repeating the same set of steps. By precisely and consistently carrying out predetermined instructions, automation software removes a large portion of this repetitive labor. Students learn how building automation projects can boost output, eliminate human error, reduce manual labor, and free workers to concentrate on more strategic and creative tasks.

Analyzing current workflows to determine whether jobs are appropriate for computer execution is frequently the first step in automation. After analyzing repetitive tasks and determining their logical order, developers write software that can perform those tasks without constant supervision. While more sophisticated systems integrate databases, online services, application programming interfaces, and cloud platforms into comprehensive automated workflows, simpler automation initiatives might rename files, organize downloaded documents, convert data types, or process spreadsheets. Automation shows how software can effectively address real-world organizational problems, regardless of complexity.

By promoting structured development methods, building projects also improve software engineering abilities. Developers learn to design application architecture, break projects down into manageable components, record critical decisions, and test functionality methodically rather than producing code at random. Because each component of the application fulfills a distinct function, modular architecture makes maintenance easier. Organization is just as vital as programming skills, since well-structured projects are simpler to understand, adapt, and expand.

Because software must operate properly in a variety of scenarios, testing is essential to the project development process. Developers verify that programs produce the desired outcomes, respond appropriately to unexpected inputs, and, when feasible, gracefully recover from errors. Testing helps programmers find flaws before consumers do and increases reliability. By enabling repeated verification whenever changes are made, automated testing methods further boost efficiency by guaranteeing that current functionality continues to function properly throughout continuous development.

Successful software projects also greatly benefit from documentation. While user documentation offers guidance on how to operate software efficiently, technical documentation discusses program design, installation processes, configuration settings, and maintenance recommendations. Well-written documentation makes it easier for future developers to understand the project and allows users to take advantage of the program's capabilities without needless misunderstandings. Establishing sound documentation practices promotes critical thinking and enhances the long-term viability of projects.

Exposing students to a variety of programming challenges and creating a variety of projects expands their technical competence. Web applications prioritize internet connection, networking, and browser technologies. Operating systems, graphical user interfaces, and local resource management are the main topics of desktop software. Automation initiatives emphasize system integration, process optimization, and efficiency. While strengthening common software engineering concepts like planning, organization, testing, security, and maintainability, each project category develops unique technological strengths.

The confidence that project development fosters through real-world success may be its greatest advantage. Completing functional applications demonstrates that theoretical ideas can be translated into practical tools that address real-world issues. Every completed project offers invaluable experience, highlights areas for development, and strengthens a developer's ability to tackle increasingly challenging tasks. Examining past work frequently reveals substantial personal development and promotes ongoing education and skill improvement in programming.

In the end, creating web, desktop, and automation projects offers one of the most comprehensive ways to hone professional software development skills. These projects create useful solutions that meet practical demands by fusing programming expertise, software engineering concepts, problem-solving skills, and user-centered design. Desktop software enhances knowledge of operating systems and graphical user interfaces, web apps educate internet technologies and global accessibility, and automation projects show how programming may boost productivity by removing tedious activities. When combined, these experiences help prospective computer scientists create dependable, manageable, and useful software that can benefit people, organizations, and communities. Students gain the technical proficiency, inventiveness, and self-assurance necessary to thrive in a field that is always changing, where real-world experience remains one of the most important pillars of long-term development and innovation, by regularly applying theoretical knowledge through practical projects.

Managing Projects with Version Control and Collaboration Practices

Since effective applications are rarely produced by a single programmer, managing projects with version control and collaborative techniques is a crucial component of contemporary software development. Development teams must coordinate their efforts effectively as software systems grow in size and complexity, ensuring that each change benefits the project. The framework for planning development, maintaining project history, reducing errors, and fostering teamwork is provided by version control systems and collaborative workflows. These procedures guarantee software quality throughout the whole development lifecycle while enabling programmers to work with confidence on common codebases.

Rather than a one-time event, software development is a continuous process. New features, bug fixes, performance enhancements, security updates, and compatibility improvements are frequently added to applications. The project's source code, documentation, and configuration files are all altered by each modification; therefore, keeping a well-organized history of these changes is crucial. Without a reliable mechanism for monitoring changes, developers can unintentionally erase crucial work, misplace earlier iterations, or struggle to pinpoint the origin of newly discovered issues. By documenting each major modification and keeping older versions for future use, version control addresses these issues.

A specific tool for tracking changes made to project files over time is a version control system. It tracks all program updates rather than just the most recent version, enabling developers to review earlier iterations, compare changes, restore earlier implementations, and understand how the project has evolved. Because it offers comprehensive details about what happened, when it changed, and why the update was made, this historical record becomes extremely useful for debugging, maintenance, and future development.

The defense against unintentional errors that version control offers is one of its biggest benefits. Programmers often explore new concepts, enhance existing functionality, or adopt alternative approaches when developing software. Not all experiments yield positive outcomes, and adding new code may introduce unforeseen errors. When needed, developers can securely revert to older stable versions without losing important work thanks to version control. Because programmers are aware that they may fix errors without starting from scratch, this capability promotes innovation and experimentation.

Collaboration between several developers working on the same application is also facilitated by version control. Programmers in charge of various aspects or components are frequently involved in modern software projects, and many of them work concurrently. Developers could unintentionally overwrite each other's work or make contradictory changes if they don't coordinate well. Each contributor can work independently and keep their modifications apart until they are ready to be incorporated into the main project, thanks to version control systems. This methodical approach minimizes confusion and the possibility of losing important contributions while increasing the effectiveness of teamwork.

One of the most helpful features of version control systems is branches. Developers can add new features, fix bugs, or test experimental concepts in a separate workspace created from a branch without affecting the main product version. The new work can be reintegrated into the primary project after it has been completed and successfully tested. This method keeps the main codebase stable and operational while enabling several development tasks to move forward concurrently. Because branching allows developers to test new ideas without jeopardizing the integrity of the production version, it also encourages experimentation.

Developers use a procedure called merging to integrate various branches. Although version control systems typically automatically integrate changes, two developers can make separate modifications to the same area of code. These circumstances lead to merge conflicts that need to be carefully examined before integrating. Comparing the opposing changes, talking about the desired behavior, and choosing the best course of action are all part of conflict resolution. While disagreements are inevitable in collaborative development, their frequency can be reduced with good communication and consistent synchronization.

Another crucial component of version control is the thorough documenting of project modifications. A meaningful statement outlining the modification's goal should be included with every recorded update, also known as a commit. Well-written commit messages facilitate future maintenance and aid developers in comprehending the rationale behind earlier choices. Professional developers offer succinct explanations of why the modification was made and how it enhances the software, rather than ambiguous descriptions. Over the course of the project, these documents develop into a significant historical resource.

Another useful teamwork technique that goes well with version control is code reviews. Other team members thoroughly review new code before it is incorporated into the main project to find mistakes, enhance readability, confirm adherence to coding standards, and, when necessary, offer better solutions. Code reviews promote knowledge sharing among team members and enhance software quality. Through productive conversations, developers expand their knowledge of software engineering principles, learn from each other's experiences, and are exposed to a variety of programming methodologies.

Communication is essential to productive teamwork. Project objectives, technical challenges, design choices, testing strategies, and development priorities are frequently discussed by software development teams. Clear communication helps team members efficiently coordinate their duties, avoids duplication of effort, and minimizes misunderstandings. Whether developers work remotely or in the same office, keeping lines of communication open promotes teamwork and guarantees that everyone is aware of the goals and direction of the project.

Organizing a project involves more than just source code. Documentation, configuration files, design diagrams, testing protocols, and user manuals are additional components of software projects. Keeping these materials up to date with the source code ensures that every part of the project evolves consistently. Organized documentation is more valuable as applications become more complicated, since it makes the project easier for new developers to grasp and enables seasoned team members to maintain the software more successfully over time.

To manage project tasks, issue-tracking systems frequently integrate with version control. Development teams maintain organized lists of defects, feature requests, improvements, and planned enhancements rather than relying on memory or casual notes. Each issue contains task-related conversations, priorities, progress reports, and descriptions. By linking code modifications to specific problems, a comprehensive record of how issues were found, addressed, and fixed during development is produced. This well-structured process enhances project management and increases visibility into overall progress.

Additionally, testing is essential to collaborative software development. Developers must ensure that the application continues to function properly, whether they add new features or alter current functionality. Tests can run automatically whenever code changes are uploaded, thanks to the direct integration of automated testing tools with version control systems. By identifying issues early, this ongoing testing reduces the likelihood that users will encounter faulty software. Additionally, developers can introduce future upgrades with more confidence thanks to automated verification.

Remote collaboration is becoming increasingly common in modern software development, enabling teams in various locations or nations to collaborate on shared projects. This is made possible by version control systems, which provide centralized repositories where developers, regardless of their physical location, can submit, review, and incorporate changes. These solutions, when paired with communication platforms and project management tools, allow companies to bring together skilled teams from all over the world while upholding uniform software quality and coordinated development standards.

Another crucial factor to consider when overseeing cooperative projects is security. Source code frequently contains sensitive data and priceless intellectual property that needs to be protected from unauthorized access. To protect project repositories, development teams employ encrypted communication, user rights, secure authentication, and frequent backups. Examining code for security flaws and making sure that private data, including passwords, is never incorrectly kept in project files are other aspects of responsible cooperation.

Additionally, collaboration techniques promote lifelong learning. Team members are exposed to a variety of programming methodologies, software design tactics, debugging techniques, and project management approaches when they collaborate with seasoned engineers. Programmers can enhance their technical proficiency and communication skills by receiving constructive criticism during code reviews and technical conversations. The development team as a whole is strengthened by this culture of shared learning, which also promotes professional development at every level of a software engineering career.

In the end, managing projects with version control and collaborative techniques is essential to producing software that is effective, dependable, and maintainable.

Version control systems facilitate experimentation, safeguard important work, maintain project history, and manage contributions from several developers. Code reviews, clear communication, well-organized documentation, issue tracking, testing, and shared development standards are examples of collaborative methods that improve teamwork and productivity while strengthening software quality. When combined, these techniques turn software development into a methodical engineering process that can handle projects of any size and complexity. Aspiring computer scientists can contribute successfully to professional software teams and create applications that are dependable, flexible, and well-organized throughout their lifecycle by learning version control and collaborative development techniques.

CHAPTER V
Advancing Toward Professional Computer Science Skills

Learning Artificial Intelligence and Emerging Technologies

Emerging technologies and artificial intelligence have become some of the most important fields in computer science, changing industries, enhancing daily life, and opening new avenues for global innovation. Intelligent virtual assistants, recommendation systems, self-driving technology, intelligent healthcare solutions, and sophisticated automation have all contributed to the progressive integration of what was previously thought of as science fiction into everyday life. In addition to artificial intelligence, other technologies reshaping the digital world include robotics, edge computing, blockchain, cloud computing, the Internet of Things, and quantum computing. In addition to training them to contribute to future advancements, learning about these technologies enables prospective computer scientists to comprehend how contemporary computing is developing. These new disciplines build on a basic understanding of programming, algorithms, data structures, mathematics, and software engineering rather than displacing classic computer science concepts, making a solid foundation crucial for long-term success.

The creation of computer systems capable of performing tasks that typically require human intelligence is referred to as artificial intelligence, or AI. Speech recognition, picture identification, language comprehension, decision-making, problem-solving, and experience-based learning are some of these tasks. Artificial intelligence systems frequently enhance their performance through data analysis and pattern recognition, whereas traditional software adheres to predetermined instructions written by programmers. AI systems are useful in industries ranging from healthcare and finance to education, manufacturing, and scientific research because of their capacity for adaptation, which enables them to perform increasingly complex tasks with greater accuracy over time.

Decades of research in computer science, mathematics, statistics, psychology, and engineering have enabled the development of artificial intelligence. In an effort to mimic logical reasoning, early AI systems mostly depended on manually set rules. These systems have trouble with tasks involving ambiguity or quickly changing information, even though they were successful at solving some issues. Researchers developed machine learning techniques that enabled computers to find patterns on their own, rather than relying solely on preprogrammed instructions, as computing power improved and vast amounts of digital data became accessible. This change greatly increased intelligent systems' capabilities and accelerated development across a wide range of applications.

Because machine learning enables software to improve with experience, it has become one of the most significant areas of artificial intelligence. Machine learning algorithms analyze data, identify patterns, and build models that can make predictions or classifications without explicit instructions for every scenario. Handwritten text recognition, movie recommendations, detection of fraudulent financial transactions, equipment failure prediction, medical image analysis, and personalized online experiences are all capabilities of these systems. Machine learning is a key driver of many current technological developments because of its ability to learn from data.

Every machine learning system is built on data. Algorithms can identify significant patterns and generate reliable outcomes when given representative, accurate, and high-quality data. However, regardless of how sophisticated the algorithm is, poor-quality data frequently results in biased outputs or incorrect predictions. As a result, one of the most crucial phases in the creation of artificial intelligence is now data preparation. Before training machine learning models, developers invest significant time in gathering, organizing, cleaning, validating, and maintaining datasets. This procedure emphasizes how crucial cautious data management is to the success of AI initiatives.

Over the past ten years, deep learning—a subfield of machine learning—has greatly advanced artificial intelligence. Deep learning models process data through several layers that can identify increasingly complex patterns, drawing inspiration from the interconnected nature of biological neural systems. Speech recognition, computer vision, language translation, medical diagnosis, and image generation have all benefited greatly from these methods. Deep learning is one of the most important technologies in contemporary AI research because of its capacity to handle extremely difficult problems, even though it often requires substantial computational resources and large amounts of training data.

The goal of natural language processing is to enable computers to comprehend and produce human language. The intricate grammar, vocabulary, context, emotions, and cultural expressions found in human speech make it especially difficult for computers to translate language accurately. Intelligent chatbots, automatic translation systems, voice-activated assistants, document summarization tools, and conversational AI platforms that can engage with people intuitively are all results of advances in natural language processing. As researchers create more complex models that can understand context and generate more insightful responses, these technologies keep improving.

Another rapidly expanding area of artificial intelligence is computer vision, which enables machines to interpret visual data. Computer vision systems identify objects and faces, monitor environments, examine manufactured goods, and help medical experts diagnose diseases by analyzing photos and video streams. Applications include scientific imaging, industrial automation, agricultural monitoring, driverless cars, and security systems. Teaching computers to comprehend visual data shows how artificial intelligence transcends mathematical computations into domains that have historically relied on human observation.

Robotics creates robots that can interact with their physical surroundings by fusing artificial intelligence with mechanical engineering, electronics, sensors, and control systems. In the fields of manufacturing, healthcare, logistics, agriculture, space exploration, and disaster relief, modern robots carry out duties. To perceive their environment, make judgments, and adapt to changing circumstances, intelligent robots employ cameras, sensors, and machine learning algorithms. As robotics technology advances, machines work more closely with people to perform physically taxing, hazardous, or repetitive tasks while enhancing productivity and safety.

Because many AI applications require massive processing power and storage capacity, cloud computing has emerged as a crucial technology supporting artificial intelligence. Organizations are increasingly using cloud systems, which offer scalable computing resources over the internet, rather than relying solely on local machines. Without having to buy pricey hardware, these platforms allow academics and developers to train complex machine learning models. By enabling remote teams to effectively exchange data, software, and computer resources regardless of location, cloud computing further streamlines cooperation.

By processing data closer to its source rather than sending it all to centralized servers, edge computing enhances cloud computing. Wearable health monitors, industrial sensors, driverless cars, and smart home systems are examples of devices that frequently need quick responses and cannot withstand network lags. By exchanging only the necessary data with cloud services, edge computing enables intelligent devices to process data locally. In settings where internet connectivity may be restricted, this method boosts reliability, reduces response times, lowers network traffic, and enhances privacy.

The Internet of Things, or IoT for short, is a network of physical devices that can exchange and gather data via communication networks. Interconnected digital ecosystems include smart appliances, industrial machinery, environmental monitoring systems, agricultural sensors, medical equipment, and transportation infrastructure. By analyzing collected data, identifying patterns, forecasting maintenance needs, and automating responses to changing circumstances, artificial intelligence improves these systems. AI and IoT work together to build intelligent settings that can increase productivity in homes, workplaces, medical institutions, and industrial processes.

Another significant new development is blockchain technology. Blockchain offers secure, decentralized ways to record transactions across distributed computer networks; it was created to support digital currencies. Blockchain, in contrast to conventional centralized databases, maintains synchronized records shared by numerous users, increasing transparency and reducing the likelihood of unauthorized alteration. Blockchain facilitates secure document management, digital identity verification, supply chain management, and healthcare record protection in addition to financial uses. Gaining an understanding of blockchain exposes students to several methods for handling data integrity, security, and trust in distributed systems.

One of the most exciting and difficult fields of cutting-edge technology is still quantum computing. At the same time, quantum computers use quantum-mechanical principles to enable more complex computing behavior; traditional computers process information using binary digits that represent either zero or one. Researchers expect significant applications in scientific simulations, optimization, cryptography, medicinal research, and materials science, even if practical quantum computing is still in the early stages of development. Understanding quantum computing helps students grasp the future direction of computational research, even though widespread use may still require major technological advancements.

As connected technologies and artificial intelligence become more pervasive in society, cybersecurity becomes more crucial. Intelligent systems often manage sensitive organizational, financial, medical, and personal data and need to be protected against misuse or unauthorized access. By detecting suspicious activity, identifying malware, monitoring network activity, and responding quickly to new threats, artificial intelligence helps cybersecurity experts. Continuous security improvement is crucial for safeguarding contemporary digital infrastructure, as attackers may also use AI to launch increasingly complex cyberattacks.

The development of artificial intelligence is heavily reliant on ethical responsibility. Decisions on public services, employment, healthcare, education, and finance are increasingly influenced by intelligent systems. Developers must ensure that AI systems operate equitably, safeguard privacy, maintain transparency, and avoid perpetuating harmful biases. Careful assessment of training data, algorithmic decision-making, accountability, and possible social repercussions are all necessary for responsible artificial intelligence. As a result, computer scientists bear a great deal of responsibility for creating systems that enhance human welfare while adhering to moral and legal requirements.

Realizing the importance of ongoing learning is perhaps the most crucial lesson in artificial intelligence and new technologies. Every year, new hardware platforms, algorithms, programming frameworks, and research findings emerge, demonstrating how quickly technology is developing. By reading up-to-date studies, testing with new technologies, engaging in technical forums, and continuously improving their knowledge, successful professionals maintain their curiosity. Since today's discoveries frequently become tomorrow's standard technology, adaptability becomes one of the most important traits for long-term success.

In the end, studying upcoming technologies and artificial intelligence gives prospective computer scientists the information they need to comprehend computing's future. While technologies like cloud computing, edge computing, robotics, blockchain, the Internet of Things, quantum computing, and advanced cybersecurity continue to expand the possibilities of software and digital systems, artificial intelligence enables machines to learn, recognize patterns, and support intelligent decision-making. Taken as a whole, these developments show how computer science transcends traditional programming to enter transdisciplinary domains that may tackle challenging global issues. Through a combination of solid foundational knowledge, ongoing education, ethical responsibility, and real-world experience, students equip themselves to make significant contributions to technological advancement while developing clever solutions that enhance lives, bolster industries, and promote societal advancement.

Strengthening Cybersecurity Awareness and Secure Development

Since digital systems today underpin almost every facet of daily life, commercial operations, healthcare, education, banking, communication, and government activities, cybersecurity awareness and secure software development have become crucial elements of contemporary computer science. The number of connected devices, online apps, and digital services is rising rapidly as technology advances, increasing both the potential for innovation and the risk of cyberattacks. Sensitive data must be shielded from unwanted access, alteration, and destruction in every computer program, website, mobile application, and cloud service. As a result, cybersecurity is no longer thought of as a specialized field exclusive to security experts. Rather, it is now a shared duty that all technology users, system administrators, software developers, and business owners need to be aware of. Aspiring computer scientists may help produce reliable software while protecting consumers, businesses, and vital infrastructure from evolving cyber threats by learning cybersecurity awareness and secure development techniques.

The term "cybersecurity" refers to a set of tactics, technologies, procedures, and practices designed to defend computer systems, networks, software, and digital data against criminal activity, unauthorized access, cyberattacks, and unintentional damage. Ensuring the availability, confidentiality, and integrity of digital resources is its main goal. Sensitive information is shielded from unwanted disclosure by confidentiality, information is kept correct and unmodified by integrity, and systems and services are always available to authorized users. Numerous decisions made during software development and system management are guided by these three principles, which serve as the cornerstone of contemporary cybersecurity measures.

Cyber threats are becoming more numerous and sophisticated as society grows more reliant on digital technology. New techniques for exploiting software flaws and compromising digital systems are constantly being developed by criminal organizations, lone attackers, political organizations, and even nation-state actors. Malware, ransomware, phishing scams, identity theft, data breaches, denial-of-service attacks, and unauthorized system intrusions are common dangers. These attacks frequently exploit flaws that could have been avoided through careful software design, secure coding practices, and informed user behavior, despite their methods and motivations varying. Developers who are aware of these risks are better able to understand why cybersecurity should not be considered an afterthought but rather integrated throughout the entire software development process.

Understanding that technology cannot completely remove all security risks is the first step towards developing cybersecurity awareness. Weak passwords, negligent handling of private data, unverified downloads, and reactions to misleading communications are all common ways that human behavior contributes to successful cyberattacks. Rather than relying solely on technological flaws, attackers often exploit curiosity and trust. Social engineering assaults, phishing emails, and fake websites all aim to trick people into divulging passwords, bank account information, or private company information. By being aware of these tactics, consumers can make well-informed decisions and reduce the likelihood that hackers gain unauthorized access.

One of the easiest yet most efficient ways to safeguard digital systems is through robust authentication procedures. Although passwords are still frequently used to confirm user identities, security risks are greatly increased by weak or frequently used passwords. Sufficient length, complexity, and uniqueness are all necessary for effective passwords to withstand automated or guessing attacks. By requiring users to provide additional verification beyond a password, such as temporary codes, biometric identifiers, or hardware security devices, multi-factor authentication further enhances security. Even if passwords are compromised, combining multiple authentication techniques significantly reduces the risk of unauthorized account access.

Designing applications with security as a basic necessity from the very beginning of planning is the focus of secure software development. Developers incorporate security measures into software design, implementation, testing, deployment, and maintenance, rather than creating software first and adding security features later. This proactive strategy lowers risks while reducing the cost and difficulty of fixing security flaws after software has been released. Secure development acknowledges that each design choice affects the program's overall security posture, necessitating careful thought throughout the software lifecycle.

Because applications regularly collect data from users, other systems, and network interactions, input validation is one of the most crucial secure coding techniques. Developers should never assume the validity or reliability of the data they receive. Rather, before processing any received data, applications ensure that all formats, lengths, and values match expectations. By rejecting unexpected or dangerous data before it reaches sensitive application components, proper input validation avoids many security flaws. This straightforward yet effective idea increases application stability while shielding software from numerous prevalent types of attacks.

Which people or systems are allowed to carry out particular tasks within an application is determined by access control. Not every user should have the same rights, especially when programs handle sensitive or private data. Developers implement authorization methods that grant permissions based on precisely specified roles and responsibilities. Customers may only access their personal data, staff may edit operational records, and administrators may change system settings. Carefully crafted access controls ensure that users interact only with information pertinent to their duties while limiting potential harm if individual accounts are hijacked.

Encryption is essential for safeguarding private data during transmission and storage. Readable data is transformed into encoded data through encryption, which can only be decoded with the proper cryptographic keys. Financial transactions, medical records, private messages, authentication credentials, and sensitive company data are all protected by encryption in modern applications. Properly implemented encryption prevents hackers from deciphering encrypted data without authorization, even if they intercept it. Encryption continues to be one of the key technologies providing secure information transmission and privacy as digital communication grows.

Encryption is only one aspect of secure sensitive data management. Developers take care to safeguard personal data, encryption keys, and authentication credentials, and refrain from unnecessarily retaining sensitive information. Passwords should never be stored in plain text; instead, they should be protected using secure cryptographic methods designed specifically to protect passwords. Unauthorized users should not be able to access configuration files that contain sensitive system information. In addition to minimizing unnecessary exposure, responsible data management reduces the impact of potential security incidents.

Software security is also greatly enhanced by error handling. Unexpected circumstances, such as incorrect input, inadequate resources, or communication breakdowns, are unavoidable for applications. Applications that are secure react politely and don't divulge extraneous technical information that might help an attacker. Applications provide user-friendly alerts while securely capturing technical diagnostics for authorized administrators, rather than presenting internal system information, specific database issues, or software configuration details. This method facilitates troubleshooting without disclosing important information to unapproved parties.

Because vulnerabilities are continually discovered throughout the life cycle of software systems, regular software upgrades are another crucial cybersecurity strategy. Before attackers can fully exploit vulnerabilities, developers offer security updates to fix them. Because known vulnerabilities are frequently publicly reported, organizations that delay fixes put themselves at needless risk. Maintaining up-to-date software versions guarantees compatibility with new technologies and security measures while also greatly enhancing security. As a result, ongoing maintenance remains a crucial duty throughout any software project.

Because testing finds flaws before applications are used by people, it is essential to secure software development. Authentication methods, input validation, access controls, encryption implementation, session management, and resistance to popular attack methods are all assessed through security testing. Code reviews, penetration testing, automated vulnerability scanners, and manual security evaluations all help identify flaws that need to be fixed. Software quality improves, and future maintenance costs decrease when security testing is integrated throughout development rather than only at the final stages of release.

By safeguarding the communication links that link users, servers, databases, and cloud services, network security enhances application security. While intrusion detection systems monitor unusual activity that might indicate an attack, firewalls control incoming and outgoing network traffic in accordance with established security policies. Transmitted data is shielded from manipulation and interception by secure communication protocols. When combined, these technologies create several defenses that reduce the likelihood of unauthorized access while enabling reliable digital communication.

Because businesses are increasingly storing data and running apps on shared infrastructure operated by cloud service providers, cloud computing raises additional cybersecurity concerns. Organizations are still responsible for properly configuring services, controlling user access, safeguarding stored data, and monitoring system activities, even though cloud platforms often offer robust security features. Understanding shared responsibility in cloud environments enables developers to build secure applications while recognizing that successful collaboration between service providers and application developers is essential to security.

Understanding the ethical obligations related to technology development is another aspect of cybersecurity awareness. Software developers frequently oversee systems that hold private financial, healthcare, educational, and personal data that affects millions of people. As a result, developers have an ethical duty to safeguard user privacy, reduce unnecessary data collection, implement appropriate security measures, and act quickly when vulnerabilities are found. One of the most important resources in digital technology is trust, and sustaining that trust necessitates a constant dedication to ethical software engineering.

Because hackers are continually devising new ways to exploit both technical flaws and human behavior, education remains one of the best defenses against cyber threats. By learning secure coding standards, taking part in training courses, practicing defensive programming, reading security advisories, and staying up to date on new threats, developers can improve their security expertise. Employers also teach staff members how to spot phishing efforts, safeguard private data, and adhere to security protocols. Cybersecurity procedures change in tandem with evolving technologies and attack techniques, thanks to ongoing learning.

Because defending contemporary digital systems necessitates collaboration between software developers, security specialists, system administrators, company executives, legal experts, and end users, collaboration further improves cybersecurity. Diverse skills and shared accountability are beneficial for security reviews, code inspections, incident response planning, and coordinated vulnerability management. Successful companies incorporate security thinking into every facet of software development and operational administration, rather than viewing cybersecurity as the purview of a single department.

In the end, building reliable digital systems that can safely assist people, companies, and society requires raising cybersecurity awareness and using secure development techniques. By combining responsible software engineering, knowledgeable user behavior, moral decision-making, ongoing education, and proactive risk management, cybersecurity goes far beyond technical tools. Through meticulous design, robust authentication, input validation, encryption, access control, testing, and continuous maintenance, secure development incorporates protection into every phase of the program lifecycle. Cybersecurity will remain an essential duty for all computer scientists and software developers as technology advances and digital systems become more interconnected. Developers may create apps that safeguard sensitive data, uphold user trust, and contribute to a safer, more resilient digital future by treating security as an essential component of software architecture rather than an optional add-on.

Creating a Professional Portfolio and Continuous Learning Strategy

Two of the most important tools for anyone interested in a career in computer science are a professional portfolio and an ongoing learning approach. Although technical expertise and programming abilities are crucial, employers, clients, and partners frequently seek concrete evidence of an individual's ability to solve problems, complete projects, and advance their career. A well-structured learning approach guarantees that knowledge stays up to date in a quickly evolving technical environment, while a well-organized portfolio highlights practical achievements. When combined, these two components provide a solid basis for long-term professional development, enabling people to pursue new possibilities, adapt to new technology, and demonstrate competence and dedication throughout their careers.

The rapid advancement of technology sets computer science apart from many other disciplines. In comparatively short amounts of time, new features are added to programming languages, development frameworks are enhanced, security procedures are altered, hardware becomes more potent, and whole new fields of expertise are created. A developer may eventually discover that crucial tools and procedures have undergone substantial change if they solely rely on knowledge gained during formal education. Throughout their careers, professionals are encouraged to continually update their knowledge, hone their skills, and explore new technologies to address this challenge. Successful computer scientists approach learning as a lifelong process that goes hand in hand with real-world experience, rather than treating education as something that ends after completing a course or degree.

A professional portfolio is a compilation of proof of an individual's technical proficiency, inventiveness, problem-solving ability, and professional development. A portfolio offers specific examples of finished work, in contrast to a resume, which provides a succinct summary of qualifications. It enables prospective employers, clients, educators, or partners to review actual projects, assess coding quality, review design choices, and understand how a person approaches software development challenges. A solid portfolio turns theoretical assertions of expertise into tangible achievements backed by real-world outcomes.

Project quality, not project quantity, is the cornerstone of any successful portfolio. Compared with dozens of incomplete or repeated projects, a small group of thoughtfully created applications often makes a stronger impression. Every project should exhibit careful planning, well-organized execution, extensive testing, and consideration for usability. The application should demonstrate the developer's grasp of software engineering concepts while resolving a significant issue, regardless of whether it is a web platform, desktop program, mobile application, automation tool, database system, or programming utility. Whenever feasible, projects should be unique, demonstrating not only technical proficiency but also inventiveness and autonomous thought.

A portfolio is strengthened by including a range of project types that show versatility in many computer science domains. Web applications demonstrate an understanding of databases, user interfaces, server communication, and internet technology. Desktop software exhibits knowledge of local resource management, graphical user interfaces, and operating systems. Automation technologies highlight efficiency, scripting, and workflow optimization. While cybersecurity demonstrations demonstrate knowledge of secure software development, data analysis initiatives demonstrate analytical thinking. Developers demonstrate their ability to adapt to diverse technical environments and project requirements by showcasing a range of experience.

Clear documentation outlining the goal, functionality, technology used, and development process should accompany every portfolio project. Reviewers can better grasp the application's functionality, design, and the rationale behind specific technical choices thanks to the documentation. The original problem, the planning process, the architecture, the difficulties encountered, the solutions implemented, and the lessons learned during development can all be covered in project descriptions. This extra context reveals intelligent engineering methods that go beyond developing functional code and showcase communication skills.

The way source code is organized has a big impact on how portfolio projects are seen. Code that is clear, understandable, and organized demonstrates disciplined programming practices and regard for long-term maintainability. Reviewers are better able to comprehend the project's implementation when there are meaningful variable names, consistent formatting, logical structure, modular design, and insightful comments. While each coder has their own coding preferences, adhering to industry norms shows professionalism and facilitates future teamwork.

Because version control history records the project's development over time, it also enhances a professional portfolio. Frequent commits with insightful explanations demonstrate well-organized development processes and the evolution of the program through subsequent enhancements. Instead of just providing a finished product, a thorough development history demonstrates that the programmer is aware of professional software engineering practices. Version control emphasizes the ability to manage change methodically, a crucial competency in collaborative software development.

Because it immediately affects how people interact with portfolio applications, user interface design merits careful consideration. If software is difficult to use or confusing, an attractive visual design is not enough. By clearly displaying information, rationally arranging features, and reducing superfluous complexity, effective interfaces strike a balance between usability and attractiveness. Consistent layouts, simple navigation, responsive controls, and accessible design principles produce positive experiences that enhance the overall perception of technical proficiency.

Another crucial component that portfolio projects should incorporate is testing. Careful verification, not conjecture, leads to dependable software. A dedication to software dependability and professional development standards is demonstrated by testing processes, whether through automated tests, written testing procedures, or evidence of quality assurance. It is also clear that software engineering encompasses validation and continuous improvement in addition to programming when testing methodologies are discussed.

Instead of remaining the same once it is created, a portfolio should continually adapt. Older projects can be improved, altered, or replaced with better examples that demonstrate current capabilities as technical skills advance. Ongoing development is demonstrated by adding functionality, strengthening security, improving user interfaces, updating documentation, and improving code quality. A dynamic portfolio conveys the idea that learning never ends, even when specific projects are finished.

Additionally, a professional presentation is crucial. A portfolio should be systematically arranged so that reviewers can easily navigate projects and find pertinent information. Readability and professionalism are enhanced by clear descriptions, uniform formatting, relevant screenshots, diagrams when needed, and easily available project demonstrations. Since first impressions frequently influence recruiting decisions, careful presentation helps guarantee that technical achievements get the recognition they merit.

By providing the knowledge needed to deliver increasingly complex projects, ongoing learning enhances portfolio development. Setting personal objectives and determining which skills are most pertinent to chosen job routes are the first steps in effective learning. While some students concentrate on web development, others study data science, artificial intelligence, cybersecurity, cloud computing, mobile applications, embedded systems, and game development. Setting specific goals enables people to prioritize their educational efforts while sustaining motivation through measurable progress.

Creating a methodical learning strategy keeps learning from becoming haphazard or uneven. Learners arrange subjects into logical sequences that expand on prior knowledge rather than studying unrelated technology aimlessly. Advanced topics such as machine learning, distributed systems, cloud infrastructure, and cybersecurity usually follow foundational ideas like programming, algorithms, data structures, networking, databases, and operating systems. This methodical approach improves comprehension while minimizing misunderstandings brought on by gaps in prior knowledge.

One of the best strategies for ongoing professional development is still reading. Learners are exposed to new ideas, programming methods, design philosophies, and emerging technologies through technical books, research papers, documentation, and industry publications. Because official documentation offers authoritative advice on programming languages, development frameworks, libraries, and software tools, it merits special attention. Developers are more equipped to embrace new technologies throughout their careers when they can independently comprehend technical documentation.

By enabling students to apply recently learned concepts right away, practical experimentation strengthens theoretical knowledge. Instead of passively learning programming frameworks, developers start with small projects that explore specific features and gradually expand these experiments into larger apps. In addition to developing problem-solving skills through firsthand experience, practical implementation highlights minute details that are often missed in theoretical study. Each completed experiment enhances the professional portfolio and builds confidence.

Open-source software offers beneficial chances for ongoing education and career advancement. Developers are exposed to real-world software engineering techniques, code reviews, version control workflows, documentation standards, and distributed teamwork through participation in collaborative projects. Professional programming methods, architectural choices, and cooperative problem-solving can all be learned from watching seasoned contributors. Students can even learn new techniques and develop their own programming style by examining open-source code from experienced developers.

By pointing out flaws that could go unnoticed during individual study, getting feedback from others speeds up learning. Teachers, mentors, coworkers, online communities, and seasoned developers can point out areas that need work and offer different approaches or more effective methods. Instead of being seen as a personal assessment, constructive criticism should be seen as a chance for personal development. Because they constantly hone their technical and communication skills, professionals who actively seek criticism frequently advance more quickly.

Effective time management has a big impact on how well continuous learning works. Daily routines, personal obligations, and professional duties frequently restrict the time available for studying; thus, regularity is more beneficial than sporadic, intense attempts. Even for brief periods each day, developing consistent learning habits promotes steady progress and keeps knowledge up to date. Sustainable learning practices promote long-term intellectual development while lowering burnout.

By enabling people to assess finished products and educational experiences critically, reflective learning further enhances professional development. After completing an application or learning a new technology, developers should reflect on what they learned, which issues proved challenging, how problems were resolved, and what could be improved in future work. Reflection strengthens decision-making skills for upcoming initiatives while converting real-world experience into enduring knowledge.

Because technology is constantly evolving, adaptability has become one of the most important traits in contemporary computer science. Programming languages change, software development techniques advance, security needs grow, and new computing platforms emerge regularly. While acknowledging that fundamental computer science concepts often endure despite evolving tools, professionals who embrace adaptability remain open to experimenting with new technologies. Throughout their careers, developers can successfully switch between several technologies thanks to their flexibility.

Continuous learning is greatly aided by networking with other professionals. People are exposed to a variety of viewpoints and new trends in the sector through technical communities, conferences, workshops, discussion groups, online forums, and cooperative initiatives. Speaking with seasoned experts often provides useful insights that cannot be found in textbooks alone. Professional connections can provide opportunities for collaboration, career advancement, mentoring, and problem-solving that enhance technical expertise and professional development.

As technology continues to impact society significantly, ethics should remain a crucial part of lifelong learning. Systems impacting education, healthcare, finance, communication, transportation, and many other facets of daily life are developed by software developers. Technical competence serves society responsibly when privacy, fairness, accessibility, responsible artificial intelligence, cybersecurity, and professional accountability are understood. Therefore, learning new technology is only one aspect of continuous education; another is developing strong professional judgment regarding its proper application.

Maintaining both a solid portfolio and an organized approach to learning is beneficial for career planning. Professionals can make well-informed career decisions by regularly examining personal goals, assessing existing skills, analyzing industry trends, and planning future learning objectives. People actively prepare for new chances by learning pertinent information before it becomes generally needed, as opposed to passively responding to technological change. During times of technological change, this proactive approach boosts confidence and fosters career resilience.

The cycle of progress that results from combining portfolio creation with ongoing learning may be the biggest advantage. While developing projects provides new information that warrants further research, learning new skills helps developers create stronger projects. Every completed application increases technical expertise, boosts self-assurance, enhances the portfolio, and reveals new educational opportunities. This ongoing cycle sustains passion for technical innovation and research while promoting lifetime professional progress.

In the end, maintaining a continuous learning plan and building a professional portfolio are crucial steps for anyone hoping to succeed in computer science in the long run. A strong portfolio shows technical proficiency, creativity, problem-solving skills, and disciplined software engineering, and ongoing education ensures knowledge stays current in an ever-changing field. When combined, these techniques equip people to confidently adopt new technologies, successfully participate in group projects, and explore a variety of employment options in the rapidly growing digital landscape. More significantly, they cultivate qualities that extend well beyond any particular programming language or software framework, such as curiosity, discipline, resilience, and a commitment to lifelong progress. Professionals who continuously develop meaningful projects, hone their skills, embrace lifelong learning, and approach their work with integrity will be well-positioned to deliver cutting-edge software solutions that benefit people, organizations, and society for many years to come as technology advances and new challenges arise.

Preparing for Careers, Freelancing, and Lifelong Growth in Computer Science

It takes much more than just learning programming languages or being proficient with technical tools to prepare for professions, freelancing, and lifetime development in computer science. While technical proficiency is still the cornerstone of any successful computer science career, flexibility, communication, problem-solving skills, professionalism, and a dedication to ongoing development are equally important for long-term success. Every year, the continuously evolving technology sector introduces new programming languages, software frameworks, cloud platforms, cybersecurity issues, artificial intelligence technologies, and development approaches. People who train for the technology of today may therefore find it difficult to stay competitive in the future. Rather, prospective professionals should concentrate on establishing solid computer science foundations while cultivating behaviors that encourage lifelong learning, professional development, ethical responsibility, and career flexibility.

Because computer technology affects almost every business, a career in computer science offers incredible diversity. Applications for businesses, education, healthcare, entertainment, transportation, finance, manufacturing, agriculture, scientific research, and government functions are developed by software developers. Network engineers create communication networks that link individuals and institutions worldwide. Cybersecurity experts defend digital infrastructure against ever more complex attacks. While experts in artificial intelligence develop intelligent systems that can solve complex problems, data scientists analyze vast amounts of data to support well-informed decision-making. Systems analysts assess corporate procedures to recommend technology improvements, while cloud engineers oversee scalable computing infrastructure. This wide variety of employment options enables people to apply common computer science concepts across professional settings while pursuing fields aligned with their interests.

Gaining a firm grasp of computer science principles is the first step towards building a successful profession. The fundamental knowledge that underpins sophisticated technologies includes programming languages, algorithms, data structures, operating systems, networking, databases, software engineering, and computer architecture. These fundamental ideas hold across technological generations, even though programming languages and software frameworks may evolve. Because they can identify the fundamental ideas shared by various technologies, developers who understand how computers process information, organize data, solve computational problems, and communicate over networks are better able to adapt to new tools.

Because companies and clients frequently consider demonstrated skill in addition to educational qualifications, practical experience is equally significant. Students can apply theoretical knowledge and gain confidence through practical problem-solving by working on real-world projects. Collaborative development activities, academic assignments, open-source contributions, internships, and personal software projects all enhance practical abilities and offer useful examples for professional portfolios. Project completion, from design to implementation, testing, documentation, and maintenance, reveals a developer's capacity to turn concepts into useful software solutions and exhibits discipline and perseverance.

One of the most important resources for computer science career growth is a professional portfolio. A portfolio offers tangible proof of technical proficiency through finished software projects, rather than relying solely on academic accomplishments or work background. Programming talents, software engineering techniques, user interface design, problem-solving ability, and attention to quality are all demonstrated by well-documented online apps, desktop programs, automation tools, mobile applications, database systems, and programming utilities. Because projects show how knowledge is applied in real-world scenarios, employers often gain more insight by assessing practical work than by reading lists of technical skills alone.

Despite the widespread belief that software development is solely a technical endeavor, communication skills are as crucial for career success. Developers frequently work with coworkers, participate in project planning, review code, provide documentation, communicate software needs to clients, and explain technical concepts to nontechnical stakeholders. Effective written and spoken communication lowers miscommunication, enhances teamwork, and fortifies bonds between coworkers and clients. Because they contribute not only through programming but also through leadership, teamwork, and problem-solving debates, professionals who can combine strong technical knowledge with effective communication often advance more quickly.

Since most professional projects require cooperation between developers, designers, testers, analysts, project managers, cybersecurity experts, and business representatives, teamwork has become a crucial aspect of contemporary software engineering. Instead of focusing solely on individual achievements, successful team members appreciate diverse perspectives, contribute positively to conversations, accept criticism professionally, and support shared project goals. Gaining knowledge of collaborative development techniques like code reviews, version control, project management techniques, and well-organized documentation equips future professionals for settings where teamwork is crucial to project success.

One of the key traits of computer science professionals is still the ability to solve problems. The real worth of a software expert lies in their ability to comprehend complex problems and create efficient solutions; programming languages and development tools only provide means of implementing solutions. Effective developers thoroughly examine requirements, assess potential solutions, foresee obstacles, and build maintainable systems that can be modified to meet changing demands. Professionals with strong analytical thinking can remain productive even as technology advances, since problem-solving techniques apply across software frameworks and programming languages.

Because digital communication allows professionals to engage with clients across regional borders, freelancing is becoming a more appealing employment option in computer technology. For firms ranging from small local businesses to multinational corporations, independent software developers may create websites, mobile applications, desktop software, automation systems, cloud solutions, or unique business tools. Flexibility, independence, and the ability to choose assignments that fit one's interests and areas of competence are all benefits of freelancing; however, as independent contractors must also handle customer relationships, contracts, scheduling, finances, marketing, and business development, successful freelancing demands far more than technical proficiency.

One of the primary difficulties faced by independent developers is establishing credibility. Demonstrating dependability is crucial because clients often have a wide range of providers to choose from. Building trust and reputation is a long process that is facilitated by a solid portfolio, favorable client testimonials, clear communication, professional conduct, and constant execution of high-quality work. Even though early freelance work may consist of very few tasks, successfully securing these opportunities often leads to larger contracts through referrals and repeat business. When building long-term customer relationships, dependability, timeliness, and honesty can prove to be just as useful as superior technical skill.

Success as a freelancer is greatly influenced by efficient project management. Independent developers must manage shifting customer requirements without compromising software quality, clearly define the project scope, communicate progress regularly, and realistically estimate timescales. Well-thought-out planning helps clients stay confident during development and minimizes misunderstandings. Successful freelancers are distinguished from those who focus solely on programming and ignore business operations by their ability to balance technical and administrative duties.

Because revenue can vary with project availability and market conditions, financial preparation is especially crucial in freelance professions. Budgets are created, emergency funds are kept up to date, business spending is monitored, and responsible specialists plan taxes, insurance, and equipment updates. Establishing excellent financial practices promotes sustained long-term career success while offering stability in between ventures. Developers are better able to concentrate on providing high-quality technical services when they are aware of the commercial sides of freelancing.

Whether a person is an independent consultant or an employee, professional ethics are always crucial. Software engineers frequently handle proprietary technology that needs to be carefully protected, financial records, personal information, healthcare information, and private company data. Professional reputations are strengthened, and confidence is fostered by upholding confidentiality, protecting intellectual property, communicating honestly, meeting contractual responsibilities, and putting user privacy first. Ethically built connections have a major long-term impact on professional achievement.

Because technological progress never stops, one of the most crucial investments made during a computer science career is continuous learning. Programming languages, cloud services, cybersecurity methods, AI frameworks, development tools, and software engineering approaches are all constantly evolving. In addition to improving their prospects across evolving industries, professionals who actively research emerging technology maintain their competitiveness. Reading technical books, taking online courses, attending conferences, participating in workshops, contributing to open-source projects, experimenting with personal software, and learning new technologies are all examples of continuous learning.

Learning shouldn't be limited to picking up new programming languages. Enhancing knowledge of fundamental topics such as algorithms, operating systems, networking, software architecture, databases, distributed systems, cybersecurity, and mathematics is equally crucial. Because sophisticated technologies usually build on these basic principles, having a solid foundation makes future learning easier. Professionals with a solid foundation in computer science are better able to adapt than those whose knowledge depends solely on specific software tools or development frameworks.

Long-term professional development is greatly aided by mentoring. When it comes to technological difficulties, career choices, workplace expectations, and professional growth tactics, seasoned developers offer insightful advice. By introducing students to real-world insights gleaned from years of business experience, learning from mentors speeds up advancement. In addition, seasoned experts gain from mentoring others, as it deepens their knowledge and benefits the broader technological community.

Career advancement is also aided by networking within professional communities. Opportunities to share information, discuss cutting-edge technology, and build deep professional connections are offered by conferences, technical associations, online discussion boards, neighborhood programming clubs, and collaborative open-source initiatives. Beyond just looking for work, networking creates environments where developers exchange experiences, collaborate to solve issues, develop creative solutions, and stay up to date on shifting market trends.

One of the characteristics that distinguishes successful computer science workers nowadays is adaptability. As industries adopt new platforms and development processes, job pathways can undergo unanticipated changes due to the constant evolution of technology. Because they approach new technology with interest rather than uncertainty, professionals who are open to change rather than oppose it continue to be important throughout their careers. Resilience is fostered by adaptability, which enables people to switch between programming languages, sectors, development approaches, and technical specializations without losing faith in their capacity to learn.

Sustaining long-term professional success depends just as much on maintaining personal well-being. Solving complex challenges that call for focus and imagination is a common part of software development. Prolonged stress, poor work-life balance, excessive workloads, and insufficient sleep can all lower productivity and raise the risk of burnout. Maintaining physical health, efficiently managing stress, creating good habits, and striking a balance between work and personal interests are all important to successful professionals. Sustainable professions rely on maintaining long-term drive, inventiveness, and general well-being in addition to technical brilliance.

When curiosity, ongoing learning, and real-world experience come together, innovation flows naturally. Professionals in computer science who frequently investigate new technologies, challenge accepted wisdom, and try out novel concepts frequently spot chances to create unique software products, enhance organizational procedures, or start their own businesses. Innovation rarely arises from solitary inspiration; rather, it develops from methodical study, careful observation, and persistent testing across a variety of technological fields.

Another characteristic that distinguishes modern computer science careers is global collaboration. While working on common software projects, development teams often come from different nations and cultures and communicate via digital media. Therefore, cultural sensitivity, courteous communication, adaptability, and respect for different viewpoints are beneficial for professionals. Collaborating with colleagues from around the world enhances professional prospects and develops teamwork abilities that are useful in a variety of work settings.

In the end, lifelong development entails more than just improving technical proficiency. Meaningful career development is influenced by a variety of skills, including leadership, communication, project management, ethical decision-making, mentoring, creativity, flexibility, and professional accountability. Many professionals move into positions in technical leadership, software architecture, education, consultancy, entrepreneurship, or organizational strategy as they gain experience. Building on years of accumulated technical expertise and real-world experience, these opportunities call for broader perspectives that go beyond programming alone.

The most crucial insight for anyone pursuing a career in computer science is probably that mastery of current technology is not the only way to gauge success. Over the course of a professional career, programming languages, software frameworks, development tools, and industry trends will all continue to evolve. The need for curiosity, disciplined learning, integrity, careful problem-solving, teamwork, and dedication to ongoing progress never changes. People who develop these traits are more equipped to deal with technological change and make constructive contributions to communities, organizations, and society.

In the end, a strong technical foundation must be combined with professional skills, ethical responsibilities, ongoing education, and real-world experience to prepare for careers, freelancing, and lifelong advancement in computer science. A strong foundation for long-term success is built by developing worthwhile initiatives, maintaining an orderly portfolio, cultivating communication skills, embracing teamwork, pursuing lifelong learning, and fearlessly adapting to technological change. Professionals who are dedicated to learning and development, whether they work as software engineers, cybersecurity experts, AI developers, cloud architects, systems analysts, researchers, entrepreneurs, or independent contractors, put themselves in a position to succeed in one of the most important and dynamic industries in the world. In addition to having prosperous careers, those who regard computer science as a lifelong journey rather than a destination are better equipped to make significant contributions that advance technology, strengthen companies, and have a positive social impact on future generations.

CONCLUSION

Rather than marking the conclusion of a single educational experience, finishing this learning journey signifies the start of a lifetime quest for knowledge. The ideas covered in these chapters offer a solid basis for comprehending how computers operate, how software is created, and how logical reasoning and methodical development can be used to address challenging issues. Every class helps develop the self-assurance, practical skills, and mindset required to keep developing in a rapidly evolving technology environment.

The abilities acquired via regular study and practical application go beyond writing code. They promote critical thinking, creativity, flexibility, and methodical problem-solving—qualities that are useful in a variety of personal and professional pursuits. One of the most crucial qualities any prospective computer scientist or software developer can have is the willingness to learn, try new things, and take on new challenges as technology advances.

Instead of following a certain educational path, progress is made via perseverance, curiosity, and constant improvement. Every project finished, bug fixed, and every new idea grasped is a step closer to being an expert. Learners can confidently pursue challenging subjects, contribute to significant technological advancements, and build fulfilling careers in the computing sector by cultivating a habit of inquiry and practical application. Anyone who is committed to learning, practicing regularly, and confidently and purposefully turning information into practical solutions can still succeed in computer science.

Thank you for buying and reading/ listening to our book. If you found this book useful/ helpful please take a few minutes and leave a review on the platform where you purchased our book. Your feedback matters greatly to us.

www.ingramcontent.com/pod-product-compliance
Lightning Source LLC
LaVergne TN
LVHW050821061126
851857LV00012B/914
9798256056063